# EVERYTHING

**YOU NEED TO KNOW ABOUT...**

# Baby's First Year

GREENWICH LIBRARIES

3 8028 01651045 2

# EVERYTHING

## YOU NEED TO KNOW ABOUT...

# Baby's
# First Year

**HELEN FRANCIS**

David & Charles

A DAVID & CHARLES BOOK

David & Charles is a subsidiary of F&W (UK) Ltd.,

an F&W Publications Inc. company

First published in the UK in 2004

First published in the USA as The Everything® Baby's First Year Book,

by Adams Media Corporation in 2002

Copyright © 2002 Adams Media Corporation

All rights reserved. No part of this publication may be reproduced,

stored in a retrieval system, or transmitted, in any form or by any

means, electronic or mechanical, by photocopying, recording or

otherwise, without prior permission in writing

from the publisher.

**Project Manager** Ian Kearey

**Cover Design** Ali Myer

ie record for this book is available from the British Library.

ISBN 0 7153 1958 2

Printed in Great Britain by CPI Bath

for David & Charles

Brunel House   Newton Abbot   Devon

Visit our website at www.davidandcharles.co.uk

& Charles books are available from all good bookshops;

alternatively you can contact our Orderline on (0)1626 334555 or

write to us at FREEPOST EX2110, David & Charles Direct,

Newton Abbot, TQ12 4ZZ (no stamp required UK mainland).

| LONDON BOROUGH OF GREENWICH | |
|---|---|
| 38028016510452 | |
| Browns Books | 30/11/04 |
| 649.122 | 9.99 |
| A0 | |

# Contents

# Introduction

As you navigate the speed bumps of parenting an infant, you might need some direction along the way. In *Everything You Need to Know About Baby's First Year*, you will find the landmarks and mile markers that let you know you and your baby are both where you need to be. Are you healing? Is he growing? Are both of you sleeping and eating enough?

This collection of wisdom from experienced mothers – first-time mums, mums of many, vegetarian mums, bottle-feeding mums and even nervous mums – will do more than help you through the challenges. It will reassure you that you – yes, *you* – have the resources to be a great mum yourself, and you should have a wonderful time doing it.

Midwives and paediatricians have contributed their expertise as well. Professional recommendations, information on what is 'normal', and a breadth of exposure support and validate the suggestions inside. It's one thing to consider a mum's opinion; it's quite another when that opinion is seconded by people who *know*.

Read on! You will find advice that is thoughtful, practical and simple, from how to survive the first few days back at home (accept all offers of help!) to what to do once your baby's mobile (brace yourself). Become familiar with ways to bathe and feed your baby, and methods for getting him to sleep. And as you're going through the suggestions, remember that 'tried and true' doesn't happen without trial and error. No one trick works for everyone.

Some of the standard soothers and entertainers, such as lullabies and nursery rhymes, are made easier because the words are right inside. Or, try one of the other suggestions for a little variety. You'll discover that even something as simple as ice cubes can keep your baby amused just long enough for you to finish your meal.

For a baby, playing *is* learning. Learn why it's better to practise games that encourage fun as much as education – you'll both be more successful. Sing, read and dance. And talk, talk, talk about this great big world!

Journal pages for your baby's development – and your own – are included, too. Track his first foods, vaccinations, even colds and illnesses, to keep things organized. And track your progress. Jot some notes on the first time you left the baby for a weekend, or how you feel about going back to work.

You see, more than anything, *Everything You Need to Know About Baby's First Year* is about you. It's about when to worry, and when to stay calm. It's about how to relax – even to spoil yourself occasionally! – and how important it is to take care of yourself, physically and emotionally.

Learn what you can ask for in the hospital and get geared up with the best baby essentials. How do you get out of the house with a new baby?

Where do you go? When is it OK to start exercising? An exercise primer will help you get yourself back in shape, and exercise is as good for the spirit as it is for the body. For extra motivation, you can even do some of the exercises with your baby!

As you prepare for (and adjust to) your new arrival, you'll find this book both useful and helpful. It's a guide and a workbook, but it's also a companion – something to help you along and remind you that you're not alone, and that many heads are better than one. It's something to remind you that there is no year like the first year – enjoy it!

CHAPTER 1

# You're a Mum!

Yesterday you were pregnant; today you are a mother. Everything has changed. Yesterday you were wondering if your baby was ever going to come out, if labour would ever end. Now, your baby is lying in your arms or in his tiny bed, and you're wondering just how much it will hurt when you finally work up the courage to stagger to the toilet.

## Don't Worry, You'll Know

You've probably spent very little time alone with your new baby. At the moment when the nurse or the midwife or your partner left the room, you also realized that along with the brand-new title of 'mother' came the expectation that you were supposed to know, well, everything. You're supposed to know how to fasten a nappy so it doesn't scratch the baby's leg or cover his umbilical cord. You're supposed to know how to tuck him into the crib so he rests on his side, just so. You're even supposed to know what the baby's colour should mean. 'Do you think he's too hot?' your partner asks you. 'He seems so red.'

'How am I supposed to know?' you think to yourself, but you don't say it. After all, you're the mum, so people think you're the expert. 'No, he's just fine,' you reply, even though you have your doubts. Maybe that last blanket *was* one too many.

But the good news is that you really are the expert – —at least as expert as anyone else when it comes to your baby. You can be sure that as you proceed through your baby's first year, what you don't know now, you will soon learn.

## Use Your Resources

Some things you'll work out with the help of your mother, your doctor or the women in the supermarket, who will be sure to give you all sorts of advice, some of it even useful. Some things you'll find out from the new friends you'll make as you struggle through the early days of motherhood. Some things you'll work out for yourself – and you'll soon share your tips with your friends. Some of the answers are in this book, collected from doctors, mothers, friends, the women in the supermarket, and my own experiences after going through three first years.

## Baby, the Extraterrestrial

A newborn baby who had a rough – or even a typical – ride down the birth canal does not look like a pink, chubby-cheeked baby. The baby often looks like something from another planet. When my third child, Mischa, was born, he weighed 4kg (9lb) and his head looked like a banana with eyes - big, bulging eyes that seemed to fill the only part of his face that hadn't been stretched to a point.

Lynne's description of her baby Clare is typical. 'She looked like a space alien, with puffy eyes and red lips. I was afraid she was ugly.'

'I thought my baby Sasha looked like a Martian,' said Natasha. 'And objective hindsight tells me I was right.'

In fact, Mischa, Clare and Sasha were normal, and your baby, as odd as he or she looks on arrival, probably is, too. Your baby may have:

- Head moulding
- A caput (a swelling on the head caused by fluid squeezed into the scalp)
- Swollen eyelids
- Flattened nose
- Floppy ears
- Fine body hair
- Swollen breasts
- Swollen labia or scrotum
- Peeling skin
- Blueish hands or feet

## Taking Care of Yourself

While much of this book will be about taking care of your baby, this first chapter is about you. You have just been through the most intense life-changing experience there is. You are stunned, exhausted, amazed, thrilled, frightened and overwhelmed. And you have to help yourself recover and adjust to this major change as soon as possible, because you have a person depending on you who isn't even aware yet that he or she isn't still part of you.

You may be one of the 99 per cent of new mothers who give birth in a hospital. You will probably stay there two days - longer if you had a Caesarian, shorter if you opt to go home early.

## Those Last Few Things

Although you'll be focused on bringing your new arrival home, there are a few things you should get together before your own departure for the hospital. As you pack for the days ahead make sure you have your toothbrush and other toiletries, warm socks and a nursing bra. You may find that prunes or prune juice, bran flapjacks and other healthy snacks will get your system back on track. Be sure to bring a notebook or journal – you'll want to make notes to yourself, or keep track of visitors and gifts. Finally, don't forget to bring the names and phone numbers of people who need to be called after the big event.

Ask your friends or family to do a phone chain or send out an e-mail on your behalf. You'll have enough to do between resting and feeding, changing and getting to know your baby.

## Social Contact

Although you may yearn for some peace and quiet, do not underestimate the importance of social contact at this time. Having a new baby can be a lonely business, especially for a first-time mother trying to cope with this new, and somewhat alien, little person. Don't forget that the maternity ward is full of women in the same position. Sharing your concerns and experiences with other mums can be immensely reassuring, and you may make some lifelong friends.

## Charing Cross Station

Even if you grab a private room and limit your visiting list, your hospital room can seem like a busy train station. Expect to see your midwife or doctor and nurses, your baby's paediatrician and nurses, a lactation consultant, and aides or volunteers who deliver food. You'll also get impromptu visits from the florist, cleaning staff and hospital administrators, as well as various repairmen who arrive just as you are falling asleep.

### Home Birth

If you've had your baby at home, your midwife will typically stay with you for several hours after the baby is born, taking both your and your baby's vital signs, cleaning up and making sure you get something to eat. She'll be back again the next day to check you and your baby, make sure breast-feeding is successfully underway, and to assess the home situation – if the house is a wreck and there is no food in the refrigerator, she'll probably suggest that you need a little more help.

## Include the Siblings

If you have an older child or children who will be visiting you in the hospital, have the new baby taken to the nursery before the older child arrives. Even if the baby is staying in the room with you, this is the time for a short stop at the nursery.

Get the older child to visit you first, to get lots of hugs and to check out your presents, flowers, and the buttons on your bed. Then send the child with your partner to the nursery to get the baby (your child can help push the movable crib down the hall). You might even want to ask the child to help return the baby to the nursery when it's time to leave. (My oldest son still talks about when he brought his new baby sister to me; I'm not sure how he thinks she got in the crib in the first place.)

## Food Time

It's hard to think about food during labour, but the minute that baby gets out, the odds are that you'll be starving – you've just completed a marathon event and your body has used every calorie available. You would think that labour and delivery nurses would come rushing in with a loaded food tray as soon as the cord is cut, but they don't. After the 3 AM birth of my first child, all the nurse could find for me to eat was a bowl of ice-cream – not the best choice, since I was shivering to begin with. (The second time I was better prepared and had a bran flapjack and a container of yogurt stashed in my overnight bag.) Bringing some food isn't a bad idea, although you may find you need to phone out for some.

## On the Menu

Somewhere between calling the world's newest grandparents and your ten closest friends, you need to get your hands on a hospital menu. You use this simple checklist to make your selections, which are delivered at the next mealtime.

'I was ravenous all the time,' said Jessica. 'On my first night I had dinner at 6 PM, and was starving at 10. I sent my husband to ask the nurse about getting more food and, to my surprise, there was none available. I found this shocking, since the entire ward was full of women who had just given birth.'

When making your choices, your first concern is for calories – you burned many more calories than you took in during labour, briefly putting your body into a state of starvation. The creation of breast milk also burns calories; you'll use about 500 calories a day more than a woman of your size who is not breast-feeding. So circle at least two items in every category on that menu. Come to that, circle anything you think you might possibly want to eat – you're better off having too much rather than too little.

Try to pick a lot of high-protein foods, since your body needs the protein to repair itself. Yogurt, milk, rice pudding – circle them all: breast-feeding mums need the equivalent of five glasses of milk a day. Look (and you may have to look hard in some hospitals) for fresh fruits, salads or vegetables. Constipation is a danger for you because your digestive system slowed down during labour and will take a while to get going again.

Beverages – tick all of them, as long as they are decaffeinated. You need to drink at least twelve 250ml (8fl oz) glasses of fluid daily to replace fluids lost during labour, keep your stools soft, prevent urinary tract infection and establish a good milk supply.

## Beyond the Menu

'I made my husband go to my favourite restaurant and get this delicious salad with balsamic tomato vinaigrette and gorgonzola cheese,' said

Natasha. 'I ate it with my fingers because I had no cutlery. It was one of the finest meals of my life.'

Ursula feels that way about the grapes she had. 'I will never buy another red grape again,' she said, 'because I want to savor the flavor of the ones I had that night.'

Lynne E sent her husband searching for Thai or Chinese food, but, because it was 1:30 in the morning and most restaurants were closed, ended up with a spinach burrito. Lynne R craved peppermint ice cream, but had to settle for a bowl of cereal and fruit.

Virginia sneaked into the hospital kitchen and took stacks of crackers back to her room, then sent her husband out for chocolate bars. Jodi drank gallons of grape juice immediately after all three of her births – odd, since she usually doesn't like grape juice. Leslie R, after swigging down a glass of crushed ice and Coca-Cola, drank a bottle of light beer. 'That would have to be my favourite bottle of beer ever,' she said, 'I had waited for nine months for it.'

## Shut-Eye

During your hospital stay your first priority should be getting as much sleep as you possibly can. For the next several months – and possibly years – your nights will not be your own. So sleep now.

## Feeling Wrecked

I had long labours. Really long. I missed one, if not two, nights of sleep while I pushed for hours. Each time my labour ended I felt like I had been in a minor car crash. I was shaking like a leaf, I had aches in muscles I didn't know I had, and I wasn't sure I was ever going to be able to walk as far as the toilet. I was exhausted, but I was also on an adrenaline rush, so sleep was out of the question for several hours. And I was starving. I knew I had about a day and a half left before they evicted me from the hospital, expecting me to walk right into my house and take care of my new baby, a thought that made me more than a little nervous. It turns out that I was pretty typical.

## Gather Your Allies

Talk to the nurses and midwifes. Tell them how much sleep you missed during the labour and how tired you are. Beg the nurses to arrange to only wake you for your baby's feedings – not to take your temperature. Nurses at some hospitals will go along with this request; others can't because it is against hospital policy. But do ask. It will help your case if your midwife or doctor makes the request as well. My second child was born in a large teaching hospital. The nurses woke me up at 2 AM and at 5 AM to feed the baby, and were back again at 6 (after I had been asleep for only 20 minutes) to take my temperature and blood pressure. Then the breakfast tray arrived at 7:15, just as I had dozed off. I don't think I got more than two hours of consecutive sleep the entire time I was there.

Lynne R was annoyed with the constant interruptions by the nurses. 'It seemed as if they came in every fifteen minutes,' she said. 'I begged them to let me get some sleep, but to no avail.'

'I got more sleep in the afternoons, when the doctors' and nurses' rounds were over,' noted Cecily.

Limit your visitors. Here, your nurses are your allies. If you begin to get inundated with visitors, tell the nurse to head them off or interrupt you after a short visit. 'On my first evening at the hospital, a friend came and stayed through most of the visiting hours while the baby was sleeping,' recalled Jodi. 'Later, when I was up most of the night, I realized I should have kicked my visitor out and slept while I had the chance.'

## Your Nurses

Your nurses are responsible for monitoring your vital signs: your blood pressure, pulse rate and temperature. Any variation from the normal might indicate the beginnings of an infection or excessive bleeding, and their primary task is to watch out for that. Follow-up care includes making sure other things are proceeding normally, including breast-feeding, the healing of your episiotomy, and the firmness of your uterus (which may need massaging).

The nurses' second most critical task is to make sure that you urinate. They will harass you about urinating at a time when you wish they would leave you alone. They will get clearly annoyed, if not hostile, if you forgetfully urinate and flush the toilet without telling anyone. Peeing may be the last thing in the world you want to do, but you have to – if you don't, you can endanger your life.

The first trip to the toilet will probably not be something you are looking forward to. It may feel fine, or it may hurt because your urethra was bruised during the birth. You may also find that once you get there you simply can't pee, either from fear of pain or because of damage to your perineum. 'The first time peeing was more painful than I expected,' said Kerri. 'I felt like I was on fire.'

You can help to avoid this burning feeling by spraying warm water (the hospital will probably give you a bottle for this purpose) while you urinate.

The first bowel movement can also be scary; your muscles relaxed during the birth and you have to push a lot harder to get a bowel movement out. After a birth the idea of doing anything like pushing seems crazy, and pushing against stitches – if you have them – does hurt.

'The first bowel movement reminds women of the pain of delivery,' says Registered Nurse-Midwife Jean Rasch, 'and women really don't want to go there.' Ask for a stool softener to take for the first few days – it can't hurt, and may help a lot.

Once you finally pee to the nurses' satisfaction, you may rarely see them again until it is time for you to leave. Because of cuts in hospital budgets, the nursing staff is overworked. But the nurses are there to help you, particularly if you know what to ask for.

In addition to the nurses, your midwife or doctor will be in to check on you, and the paediatrician will check your baby, to make sure that the baby appears normal physically and that there are no gross deformities, heart problems or physical concerns that are easily corrected if detected early (such as 'clicking hips'). The paediatrician will also evaluate breast-feeding – how it's going so far, whether you are nursing frequently enough (regardless of whether your milk is in yet), and will recommend a lactation consultant if necessary.

## Getting Ready to Go Home

Many women are desperate to leave hospital and start family life at home, while some don't want to leave the reassuring environment of the ward. However you feel, don't be shy about talking to your midwife or nurses. Discharge policies vary between hospitals, but as long as there are no medical contraindications, you may be allowed to go home after just a few hours – especially if this is not your first baby. If you gave birth naturally you are unlikely to stay in for more than 48 hours, although you can expect to stay longer after a Caesarean.

Remember that giving birth was a momentous emotional, as well as physical, experience. Talk through your feelings about the birth with your midwife or partner. Once you get home you may feel a bit abandoned, but remember that your midwife will visit you at home for the first ten days and then hand over to your health visitor. This may also be a good time to get to know the other women who were in the maternity ward with you – they can be a great source of support.

**How can I ease the pain from an episiotomy?**
Unfortunately, the wound will become more painful before it feels better, as the area swells and the stitches get tighter. Sitting on an inflatable rubber ring may help. Take warm baths and showers and do your pelvic floor exercises – even if you don't feel like it, as this encourages healing. Many women find ice packs very soothing – ask your midwife for advice.

## Easing Perineal Pain

Premoistened witch hazel pads help with the swelling as well. Get a jar from the nurse and use them to line your sanitary towel, or put them on top of an ice pack. If you're really sore, you can ask for a topical anaesthetic and squirt a blob of foam onto the pad. If you're still sore when you get home, try pouring witch hazel on a few of your maternity sanitary pads (get them thoroughly damp, but don't completely soak them) and freeze them. Mums say these super ice packs are fantastic for relieving perineal pain. You can also soak square gauze pads in witch hazel and refrigerate them.

## Yes, It Hurts

You will hurt. You don't push something as big as a newborn baby out of as narrow a passage as your vagina without incurring some damage. You may have experienced a natural tear or had an episiotomy and the stitches in your perineum may pull and itch. You may have made it through without stitches but have bruised labia. And you may have aches and pains where you never expected them, from your thigh muscles, if you stood during labour, to your chest muscles, if you had a hard time pushing. You may have haemorrhoids.

**Laborade:**

This home-made mixture, recommended by some midwives, is designed to alleviate post-labour exhaustion. Make it in advance.

> In a blender combine:
>> 80ml (2½fl oz) fresh lemon juice
>>
>> 80ml (2½fl oz) honey
>>
>> ¼ tsp salt
>>
>> 2 calcium-magnesium tablets, crushed
>>
>> enough water to bring total to 1 litre

'My episiotomy was swollen, filled with fresh blood after the wound began bleeding again, and re-sutured – a real mess,' said Virginia. 'When I stood up for the first time, I thought that my bum would fall out.'

The sensation of feeling your insides sag is a surprising one, and one that actually won't ever go away completely. While you never really noticed before the birth, looking back you may recall that your insides always felt snug. Now they don't. But you'll probably adjust to that feeling as being normal. (Except, as I recently found out, when jumping with your kids on a trampoline. Then that sense of everything threatening to fall out of your vagina comes rushing back.)

## Haemorrhoids

Haemorrhoids are swollen veins around the rectum that are typically caused by pressure, such as carrying and pushing out a baby. Many new mums have haemorrhoids; the good news is that, in most cases, they do go away. The bad news is that, while present, they can make having a bowel movement, or even sitting down, extremely uncomfortable. To find relief:

- Avoid constipation. Drink lots of water, walk around, eat fresh fruits and vegetables, take a stool softener.
- Soak in a warm bath or hip-bath.
- Sit on an inflatable cushion to relieve pressure until the haemorrhoids heal; take the cushion around with you – it beats standing all the time.
- Use over-the-counter remedies, which include refrigerated bottled witch hazel, and hydrocortisone cream.

## The Painful Truth

You may feel pain in your coccyx, which can take a pounding during a vaginal birth. It may be bruised, in which case the pains will go away after a month or so, or it may be dislocated. (I discovered this when my coccyx pressed on a nerve and I lost all the feeling in my right leg. A chiropractor was able to fix it, although it still slips occasionally.) Stretching can also help make your coccyx feel better.

Afterpains, which are cramps as your uterus contracts, aren't usually so bad the first time around, but the strength of them can be a surprise to second-time mums. This is the time to reach for a painkiller, typically acetaminophen, ibuprofen, or a narcotic such as Tylenol with codeine, hydrocodone or oxycodone. Paracetamol and Ibuprofen have few side effects and are generally considered benign. All the narcotics can cause dizziness, nausea and vomiting. Codeine and Percodan can also increase constipation. If you are breast-feeding, talk to your doctor about your pain-relief options.

You will also bleed – more than you ever imagined – and that's normal. (But if you're still soaking a thick maternity pad every hour after the first three hours you should alert the nurse, or, if you're at home, call your doctor or midwife.) You may have bruises on your face and chest. You may be sweating, as your body sheds the extra fluids it stored during pregnancy. You also may have some odd symptoms – mums have reported itchy rashes that can appear anywhere on the body. (The reason for this is not clear, but it is not uncommon, and the rashes go away on their own.) None of these are anything to worry about.

These symptoms could indicate a uterine infection, which can be life-threatening:

- Fever above 38°C (100.4°F) (measured orally)
- Blood clot larger than a walnut
- Bad-smelling discharge
- Pain when urinating that gets worse as time passes instead of better
- Pain in calf or thigh without redness
- Pain or reddened and tender area on breast

## All Shook Up

Shaking can accompany any type of delivery, vaginal or Caesarian, as the body restabilizes after the loss of blood and other physiological stresses.

Leslie B remembers the shaking well. 'I was unable to stop for quite a while,' she said. 'I watched as the paediatrician checked out my daughter and the nurse gave her a bath. I was anxious to hold her, but I was shaking so much I didn't want to chance it.'

### Breathe Easily

After the birth of my children, who tended to the hundredth percentile in head size and therefore didn't pop out with a couple of pushes, I typically found that I was short of breath. This was particularly true after my second child, and the nurses didn't know what to make of it.

However, the hospital was running a pilot programme on postpartum massage, making a masseuse available at a nominal fee. I made an appointment. After a one-hour massage, my breathing returned to normal. It turned out that all the pushing had caused my chest muscles to spasm. The massage also eased the cramp in my thighs and a lot of other aches and pains that were making it a difficult to sleep well. So I'm in favour of the necessity of a postpartum massage (although hot showers will help, too) as soon as possible.

After the birth of my third child I brought in my own masseuse – some hospitals allow this, and some masseuses specialize in pre- and post-pregnancy massage. Ask around, find someone's name, and have a masseuse on call. (You might suggest this as a nice gift from a relative who would otherwise send flowers.)

## Exercise

After nine months of pregnancy, you probably don't want to hear this, but it is time to start doing your pelvic floor exercises again – you can do them before you've even left the delivery bed. At first, you won't feel anything; it won't even feel like you have any muscles there, but keep trying every few hours, and eventually you'll get a response.

**How do I do pelvic floor exercises?**
Tighten all the muscles around your urethra, vagina and anus, hold tight for three seconds, and release. The best time to do this is when you are urinating, and you'll know you are doing it right when you shut off the flow of urine. Repeat 20 times, twice a day.

Pelvic floor exercises increase the blood flow to the vaginal area, which will help healing, and will tone up the muscles that keep you from peeing when you laugh. (These muscles will also come into play when you eventually think about having sex again – see Chapter 19.)

As soon as you can, get up and walk around. This stimulates your digestive and circulatory systems (which are probably sluggish after the birth), prevents blood clots and starts the general recovery of your muscles. Your first walk, however, may be a challenge. 'The first time I got up and walked around I felt like my insides were going to fall out and my legs were going to buckle,' said Cecily. You may not want to, but go for a walk anyway.

## Post–Caesarian

Mums who are recovering from a Caesarian often don't have perineal pain, although some may if they try to push. The primary pain is at the incision; this can be exacerbated by the internal pressure of trapped wind created when the digestive system is slowed by anesthesia and other drugs.

You can reduce wind pains by getting up and moving as soon as possible (shuffling slowly down the hospital hall counts, so don't try to do too much). Pressing a pillow against your incision as you climb out of bed can reduce the pain of getting up and moving.

# There Is Always Paperwork

By law you have to register the birth of your baby within 42 days of the birth date (21 days in Scotland). It's worth thinking about early, as time just disappears once you are at home with a new baby. Births must be registered in the district in which the child was born, although you can visit any registrar in the country to arrange this. If you are having a hospital birth, ask if you can register the birth there before you leave.

If you are married, either parent can register the birth – this also applies if you were married at the time of conception but are not at the time of the birth. If you are not married, the father and mother must register the birth together in order for the father to be named on the birth certificate. If the father cannot attend, he may make a statutory declaration of paternity, which the mother must take to the registrar. If only the father can attend, the mother must make a similar declaration of the paternity. If this applies to you, ask the registrar for a form when you book your appointment. The registrar will be happy to advise you if you have any queries regarding your circumstances.

If, for whatever reason, the father is not recorded on the original birth certificate the birth can be re-registered at a later date – ask your registrar.

You don't have to take your baby with you to see the registrar – the hospital or health authority can confirm the birth details based on the information you provide.

# CHAPTER 2

# Home Sweet Home: The First Days

The nurses and midwives gave me lots of advice as I was leaving the hospital, most of which I didn't remember. However, there was one important rule I did follow: 'When you get home,' my midwife told me, 'change immediately into a nightgown and dressing gown, and don't put on outdoor clothes for seven days.'

## So Here We Are

My husband and I left hospital at 9 PM on a Saturday night, some 45 hours after our first son was born. It took us about half an hour to fumble tiny Alexander into his going-home babygrow, and almost as long to work out how to adjust the car seat and strap him into it. The strangest part, however, was walking into our empty house, having left it only two days earlier, with the sense that so much had changed. Once we worked out how to get Alexander out of the car seat, we weren't sure we knew exactly what to do with him.

That awareness of yourselves as new parents sets the stage for how you are going to handle the job of being a parent and relating to your child. As nice as it might be, do not have relatives come and stay in your house for the first week after you bring your first baby home. This is an important time for parent/infant bonding, and privacy is necessary for the parents to develop competence and confidence.

## Gifts for Mum

Your family and friends may ask what they can do to help. The best gifts during these early weeks may be daytime visitors who come in, do some cleaning, cooking and laundry, and then quietly go home or back to their hotel. Ask someone to take the older children out for an afternoon, or bring in a home-cooked meal. (Roast chicken is perfect for hot or cold leftovers, bone-picking and soup.) Other useful gifts are a cordless phone to keep near the nursery or gift certificates to local restaurants that do take-away meals.

Whether it's going to the post office, dry cleaner or video store, someone else can do your errands. Once you know that your house and home are being cared for, you'll be able to relax. Then you'll have time to enjoy your flowers, look at the cards and bouquets that are delivered, and think about all the people who love you and your baby.

## Rules for Your First Week at Home

Your partner will have to help you out here, but this is the time to concentrate on yourselves and your family. Rest and privacy are necessary for both your and your infant's well-being.

In case not everyone was on the phone chain, record a baby announcement on your answering machine, and then unplug the phone. 'I wish I had had more time with the baby and made a few less phone calls,' Natasha said. 'Although it's tempting to call everyone and tell them about the experience, those calls can wait; the opportunity to spend time with the new baby doesn't come again.'

Don't sit down without something to drink in front of you – especially if you're breast-feeding. It's important to stay well-hydrated, for your sake and your baby's. You should try to take at least two naps a day, but keep in mind that sleep is also dehydrating.

**How can I politely discourage visitors?**

Not answering the door is awkward and makes you feel like you're hiding in your own home. Worse is a door that's knocked on repeatedly, or a doorbell that's rung continuously. In order to politely preserve quiet and privacy hang a simple note on your front door explaining that mum and her new baby are sleeping. Ask the person to not knock or ring at all, in fact, but let them know where they can leave deliveries.

Try to limit your visiting hours. Friends and neighbours may come bearing gifts or food. Graciously thank them, explain that you're too tired for company, and say you look forward to seeing them over the next several weeks. 'The best advice I was given – but didn't take – was to limit visitors for the first week or two,' Cecily said. 'Since I didn't, I felt like I didn't have time to lock into the baby's needs, but was rather trying to work the baby's needs around my visitors.'

The best way to ensure that you do rest and spend time alone with your baby is to stay in your nightgown and dressing gown. As Kerri said, 'A good friend told me not to shower and get dressed, because once you do that, people won't wait on you. I showered, and was cooking and cleaning. I should have stayed in my dressing gown and milked it for as long as I could.'

Living in a nightgown for a week (I had two that would work for nursing, and just kept washing them) has several purposes. First of all, it reminds you - and everyone else – that the most important thing you can do for yourself at this point is rest and let other people take care of you. You're a lot less likely to want to do chores around the house or run an errand if you're in your nightgown, and people (like your partner) are less likely to expect you to do anything more than feed your baby. (Someone else should be changing the nappies for now.) 'My biggest mistake was not taking care of myself enough,' Alissa said. 'When flight attendants on planes tell you to put on your own oxygen mask before helping your child, they are right. I understand that better the second time around.'

When to call the doctor:

- Very high or very low temperature
- Refusal of several feeds in a row
- Yellow eyes and jaundice (yellow skin) down to the toes
- Inability to wake baby for a feeding after six hours of sleep
- Abnormal breathing
- Blue colour around lips
- Any unusual rash
- Significant amount of vomiting or diarrhoea

## Feeling Better Every Day

If you're still having perineal pain, ask your partner to keep those ice packs coming. Or find a discreet patch of sun and expose your perineum for a few minutes a few times a day to help it heal more quickly. You can also run a shallow bath, or use your or baby tub. If you have an inflatable rubber ring, use it as a cushion in the bath.

## Six-Week Check-up

Six weeks after the birth, both you and your baby will be given a check up at the hospital or your GP's surgery.

The doctor will check your blood pressure, weight and take a sample of your urine. She will also examine your breasts and abdomen, and any stitches you had. You will be given an internal examination to check that your uterus is returning to its original position and size.

The doctor will check the baby's weight and length (approximate, as babies don't often co-operate by lying still and straight!), eyes, hearing, muscle tone, hips, head circumference and control, and check for heart abnormalities. She will also check the baby's reflexes.

## Herbal Remedies for Postpartum Relief

Several of these herbal remedies can provide simple comfort for you now, and are always helpful to have around.

*Aloe vera gel* (fresh, from a plant) cools your skin, relieves pain and helps healing. Squeeze the gel from a leaf onto your sanitary pad.

*Catnip tea* relieves afterpains and relaxes nervous tension.

*Comfrey (leaf or root) tea* builds new cells and relieves pain from perineal cuts or tears and hamorrhoids. Drink it or use it in a hip-bath.

*Ginger* soothes stitches from a Caesarean. Soak a clean cloth compress in an infusion made of boiled water and grated ginger.

*Golden seal* infusion prevents infection and relieves pain. Use it in a hip-bath.

*Slippery elm bark* soothes pain from perineal tears and strengthens the skin. Make a paste combining the powder, water and olive oil, and spread directly on tear.

## Hello, Stranger

Your priority during these first days is getting enough rest. The only way you can recover physically, establish your milk supply and bond with your baby is if you are well rested. This is a special time – preserve it.

It's also time for your body to adjust to its new role. Your hormone levels are shifting and adjusting again, you're healing, you're up at all hours, you're excited and maybe you're nervous, too. Simply – you're tired.

If you burst into tears, go to bed. If you're still crying after you wake up, call your doctor; you may need medical help to cope with depression while your hormones slowly return to normal.

I remember yelling at my husband, who stayed home from work for the first week, to stop phoning his office and put away his tools.

'You mean, you want me to just sit here?' he said, amazed, having looked at this week at home as a chance to get a few things done around the house.

'Exactly,' I replied, because any activity that wasn't related to the baby seemed like a rude interruption.

After a week or two in your dressing gown, take the baby for walks in the buggy or sling. The exercise will improve your mood, the motion will settle your baby down, and everyone you meet will coo at the baby and fuss over you, which can give you an ego boost when you need it most.

What my husband should have been doing (and eventually did do – and your partner should, too) was to keep guard over intrusions into this milky, sleepy baby space. That means your partner should set and limit visiting hours, field phone calls, and manage all the details of daily life (from paying bills to replacing the toilet paper) so you can focus just on the baby and your recovery. Because all too soon, reality returns.

## The Birth Experience

Your hormones aren't the only things adjusting themselves. Perryn Rowland, a registered maternity teacher, says, 'As a labour assistant, the most important thing I do for postpartum mothers is help them process the birth experience. This is a major event, and you need to talk about it. You need to reminisce about how you were feeling when this nurse walked in, laugh about how cross you got with your husband, and go over the birth in detail.

'And the dads need to talk about what they were experiencing. Because only after you talk about this tremendous thing that you both went through, only after you process the birth, can you move on and meet the next challenge.'

Buy a journal or a notebook, or even record your impressions in your baby book. Listening to your partner and seeing your story in your own words will add a whole new dimension to your experience.

## Still Eating for Two

If you're nursing, you need at leasat three good meals a day, and about 500 extra calories a day. For an average woman, that adds up to 2,700 calories a day. Include eight 250ml (8fl oz) glasses of non-caffeinated fluid. If you drink when you're thirsty and your urine is light in colour, you know your fluid intake is adequate.

Keeping up your calcium intake is important; you need a total of five glasses of milk or calcium equivalents a day. Insufficient calcium won't affect your milk supply, but your body will raid its own calcium stores to make up the difference, weakening your bones and teeth. (If you keep up your calcium intake after weaning, your bone mass will return.) It doesn't take milk to make breast milk; if you are allergic to dairy products, eat plenty of green, leafy vegetables and make sure you're getting enough other fluids.

Stick to decaffeinated coffee or limited amounts of regular coffee. The amount of caffeine that gets into breast milk is small, but do you really want to risk making your baby wake up more often? You can eat all the garlic you want – the flavour does get into your breastmilk and, much to the surprise of the researchers who decided to study this, most babies like the taste and nurse better.

You'll quickly learn that you shouldn't go far without bringing a drink and a snack along. Says lisa, 'My husband has brought me just over four million bottles of mineral water since I started nursing. He is my nominee for sainthood.'

## Beyond the First Days

Here are the top 20 favourite treats for new mums:

20. A haircut that camouflages hair loss
19. Sleeping late in the morning while dad takes the kid/s
18. A girls' weekend away
17. A jacuzzi
16. A day at a health farm
15. An afternoon film
14. Painting classes
13. A girls' night out
12. A silent pedicure with a book
11. Dancing
10. A new outfit that fits your body right now
 9. Doing yoga
 8. Coffee (or a decaffeinated drink if breast-feeding) alone
 7. Going out with your partner
 6. Someone else cleaning your house
 5. Being home alone in a clean house
 4. A massage
 3. A long shower
 2. A long, hot bath
 1. Sleep, sleep, sleep

CHAPTER 3

# Let's Talk Sleep

When you walk down the street, pushing your baby in a buggy, and stop to exchange coos with another mother, you don't want to know what book she's read recently or if she's seen the latest Hugh Grant movie. You want to know how much her baby sleeps. (And of course it's probably more than your baby does.)

## Sleeping Position

You have been inundated with literature about babies' back sleeping by now, so I won't labour the point. However, it's important to repeat that doctors and experts recommend that healthy infants be placed on their backs to sleep, as recent studies have shown that back sleeping is related to a lower incidence of cot deaths, or sudden infant death syndrome. So you absolutely should put your baby down to sleep on her back.

**What is positional plagiocephaly?**
Positional plagiocephaly is the flat spot on your baby's head that may develop if he always sleeps in one position. Try to get your baby to vary which side of his head rests on the mattress when he is asleep. During the day when he is awake and supervised, make sure you put him down on his stomach occasionally.

## In the Beginning

When you first bring your baby home from the hospital, she will sleep an average of 15 hours a day, generally in random chunks throughout the day and night. (Note: Your baby may sleep almost all the time, or as little as 11 hours or less.) Your baby may be at his most alert at 2 AM and apparently have no interest in going back to sleep until 4 AM. This day/night reversal is not unusual. While you were pregnant, your baby probably did a lot of his sleeping during the day, when you were walking around and rocking him with your movements, then got more active as soon as you put him down for the night.

## Finding a Rhythm

You can begin to teach your baby that it's much more fun to be awake during the daytime than it is at night. If your baby was in the nursery at the hospital, day differed little from night – lights on, babies crying, people moving about 24 hours a day. At home, though, you can make day and night distinct. Try waking your baby up every two hours in the afternoon, and whenever he's awake during the day, make it fun time. Talk to him, get out those baby toys, take him outside to listen to the birds, and introduce him to visitors.

*f@ct*

The 'average' baby (of course, no baby is actually average) will sleep each day for:

- 16½ hours at one week
- 15½ hours at one month
- 15 hours at three months
- 14¼ hours at six months
- 13¾ hours at one year

At night, don't talk to him much, don't turn on anything brighter than a nightlight, don't play with him – don't even change his nappy unless it's dirty or soaking through. In time, most babies will welcome nighttime with their longest chunk of sleep – as much as four or five hours. (Realistically, though, you probably won't go to bed the minute your baby does, so you still won't be getting nearly as much sleep as you need.)

By the end of the third month, he should be doing the bulk of his sleeping at night. (But still not, unfortunately, in long enough stretches to make you feel like you've really slept.)

## Sleep Deprivation

After three months, the sleep deprivation will start to tell on you, and you will begin to wonder if your baby will ever sleep through the night. The effect of sleep deprivation is much more pronounced than being simply tired. While you may notice delayed reaction times, clumsiness, and blurred vision, you may be too exhausted to notice impaired reasoning and judgment, apathy and agitation, and an increased sensitivity to pain.

In addition to being forgetful, confused and increasingly irritable, you will seriously start to resent the mothers of babies who are sleeping from 7 PM to 7 AM (you *will* meet these people), and wonder if you're doing something wrong. You're not. They just drew good cards for this hand and have kids who like to sleep. If you're one of those, you can skip the rest of this chapter; save your energy for the next challenge your child throws at you. (But try to keep quiet about the amount of sleep you're getting; the rest of us really don't want to hear about it.)

**Does sleep affect breast-feeding?**
Rest is important; if you don't rest enough, your milk supply will decrease. Then you'll get even less sleep because your baby will be hungry and wake more often.

For me, the magic number is five. If I have five consecutive hours of sleep, and a few more hours of interrupted sleep, I am a reasonably sane person. I can remember where I put my car keys, walk without tripping, and usually carry on a rational conversation. But if I go weeks at a time without that five-hours of sleep, I start having problems. When my daughter was a wakeful newborn baby, I towelled my four-year-old son dry, then struggled to tape a newborn-size nappy around him, annoyed because for some reason the silly thing didn't fit. I'm not sure why he stood so quietly as I struggled – either he was shocked into silence, or he was afraid that if he stopped me I might try something really crazy.

So, the issue isn't how much sleep your baby is getting – it's whether you are getting enough hours of sleep to cope as a parent, and how many of those hours are unbroken. Only you know how much sleep is 'enough' and how best you can get it. If you are dangerously sleep-deprived and your baby will drink from a bottle, try spending an occasional night sleeping (alone) on the couch of a childless friend while your partner handles night duty. One night's rest can make all the difference.

## Sleep Strategies

Now, can those of us not blessed with sleeping beauties do anything to get our babies to sleep just a little longer? Maybe. There are plenty of programmes to choose from; some may work for your new baby, and then not work for your next one. Some may seem remarkably sensible to you, but to someone else they may seem crazy.

Before exploring the different programmes described in Chapter 4, let's look at the relative importance of sleep issues. You may read that it is important for your baby to learn to fall asleep by herself because learning this will make her self-reliant. Personally, I don't think so. I don't think my kids were less confident about their ability to slither down a slide on their own or had a harder time separating from me on their first days at playgroup because I didn't teach them to fall asleep alone by the age of six months.

You may also read that babies will sleep more soundly if alone in a crib, but your baby will get plenty of sleep even if you're sitting up holding him all night. Actually, he'll sleep just fine that way.

*fact* Turn off the lights when you put your baby to sleep at night. Babies typically don't become afraid of the dark until the age of two, so until then, why start the nightlight habit?

## Tried and Tested

In addition to structured sleep methods, there are some simple practices that just work. Like any method, they won't work for all babies, but they're helpful and may work for yours. When your baby is a newborn, let her fall asleep in your arms, then gently put her down in the cradle or crib, keeping one hand on her chest the whole time. Place both hands on her for a moment after she's down, then lift them very slowly. Keeping your baby awake when he's tired during the day will not make him sleep better at night – it will just make him more fretful. Nap timing does have an effect, however, and you'll be much better off if your baby takes an afternoon nap than if he stays awake all afternoon and falls asleep at 5 PM. Don't worry about building a bad habit in a baby under three months old –if it works for tonight, it's good enough!

You don't have to turn your house into a public library when your baby is sleeping – let the radio play, the dishes clatter, and the doorbell ring. He'll quickly learn to sleep through the noise, and you'll be able to relax instead of tiptoeing around.

## The Real World

In the real world, mothers are reading stacks of books about sleep, talking about it with their friends, and then doing whatever works for them. Sometimes, of course, they don't tell anybody about it, feeling guilty that they aren't following the rules. 'Yes, my baby is sleeping through the night,' a mum you meet at the park will tell you, not bothering to mention that her definition of 'through the night' is from midnight to 4 AM.

### Gearing Up

While sleep specialists may laugh at mums who fill shopping carts with sleep aids, from automatic crib vibrators to tapes of ocean sounds, some mums have reported success with a number of products.

Motion is usually effective, so look for anything that keeps your baby rocking or gently bouncing. In addition to a baby bouncer or rocker, try holding the baby while bouncing on an exercise ball. Sitting and bouncing will also be more restful for you, and beats pacing the floor.

If you need a hands-free method, a wind-up swing or vibrating bouncy seat will soothe him to sleep. Keep him in the kitchen while you're cooking, or rest the seat on a tumble drier (but don't leave her without supervision). The constant hum might work on your baby. Get a tape player that reverses automatically, and stock up on cassettes of lullabies or your own favorite soothing tunes.

And if all else fails, there's always driving. Rumbling bumps, a rocking motion and the running engine combine the best of everything. It can be wildly impractical, or you may find it relaxing – my favourite baby-sleep drive was to the ocean, where I'd park facing the waves and get out a book.

CHAPTER 4

# Sleep Programmes

When you're trying to decide what to do about your baby and sleep, consider what will work for you, and what will work for your baby. Don't worry that you're stuck once you make your choice. If you're like most of us, you'll try a few methods, settle on one for your first child, and then find that it is completely ineffective for your second.

## Sleep Basics

There are a few rules that many – but not all – of the programmes share. If you don't want to go all the way with any one approach, you might start with these elements as you work out a system of your own:

- Try to put your baby down to sleep when he is drowsy but awake. This may teach him to put himself back to sleep when he wakes up.
- Establish a pre-bed ritual and don't vary from it. Make sure it is of a reasonable length and includes books or songs that you won't be tired of for years to come. (I've been singing my daughter to sleep with four Christmas carols since Christmas 1995, and it's getting pretty boring.)
- Get your baby attached to a 'lovey', also known as a 'transitional object'. The idea here is that the baby will look for the lovey when she wants to calm down. Some people do question whether you want your baby to bond with you, the mother, or with a yellow duck, but when you absolutely can't be there, lovies really come in handy.
- Don't do anything. Your baby will eventually sleep through the night – at least some time before he's a teenager, at which point your problem will be dragging him out of bed before noon.

If you want to encourage your baby to become attached to a lovey, nudge her towards something that can be purchased in bulk, for when the original is lost or mislaid.

## Ferberizing

In the programme proposed by Richard Ferber in his book *Solve Your Child's Sleep Problems*, the goal is for the baby to learn to put himself to sleep alone in a crib, and then to put himself back to sleep without a fuss when he wakes up during the night. This is a positive experience that gradually teaches the child to fall back on his own resources for comfort.

Ferber likens the process to what an adult would have to go through should he be forbidden to sleep with a pillow. At first he'd have trouble falling asleep and would wake repeatedly, but, after a few nights, he'd get used to it and sleep just fine.

Ferber's system, like many others, starts with a bedtime ritual (a bath perhaps, followed by a book or a song). You or your partner then put your baby to bed while the baby is still awake. The parent leaves the room (and the baby cries). The parent returns in 5, then 10 then 15 minutes, and at subsequent 15-minute intervals, to reassure the baby. The parent does not stay in the room, rock the baby or give him any 'crutches' (such as a bottle or a dummy). And, no matter what, the parent does not take the baby out of the crib. This is repeated every time the baby wakes during the night. Starting on the second night, each interval is extended by five minutes.

While Ferber offers gradual alternatives (sitting next to the crib in a chair, for example, and moving the chair farther away every night), the approach of leaving for timed intervals is the one he most recommends.

Ferberizing may go on for hours a night, for days or even weeks. It usually works eventually. The big question is whether or not you are able to make it to the 'eventually'. (In most cases, dads have an easier time sticking to this programme; the hormones released in nursing mothers when listening to a screaming baby for an extended period of time do not make things any easier.)

Since Ferber's book came out, a number of similar but slightly modified plans have been published. Probably the best news is that recent research has shown that you don't need to repeat the Ferber process each time the baby wakes up during the night. Do it once at the beginning of the night, and then go ahead and rock him to sleep when he wakes up. In most cases, that won't delay the onset of the era when the baby finally sleeps consistently through the night.

## Family Bed

Parents, babies and young siblings sleeping together in the family bed is the way babies have slept throughout most of history – and still do in much of the world. In the Western world today, it has become popular again as one of the tenets of a childrearing philosophy called 'attachment parenting'. The family bed is extolled by William Sears in *Nighttime Parenting* and *The Baby Book*. Sears says that babies sleep differently than adults, with more waking periods and longer periods of light sleep, for a reason – they need to be able to wake easily when they are hungry or cold, or when their breathing is compromised.

The family bed has several benefits beyond the closeness and awareness it fosters between you and your baby. You may find it easier to get your baby to sleep on her back, and your sleep cycles will become synchronized. When you do wake up, it will be out of a light sleep rather than a deep one, and soothing or feeding her will be that much easier.

These suggestions for preventing SIDS are culled from several studies, conducted by consultant paediatricians:

- Get good prenatal care
- Make sure the mattress of the crib or bed fits tightly into the frame, and use tight-fitting sheets
- Ban stuffed animals, pillows, and quilts (use a cellular blanket)
- Don't overheat the baby by overdressing or keeping the room too warm
- Always keep the baby in a nonsmoking area
- Breastfeed
- Put your baby to sleep on her back

Putting your baby in a crib has its own benefits. You may find that you sleep better with more room and without a squirming, kicking bundle beside you. If you can't sleep for fear of squashing the baby, or if you have a panic attack every time she makes a noise, you won't sleep at all or function well when you're supposed to be awake.

Sears suggests nursing or rocking the baby into a sound sleep before putting him down, either in a cradle or the parents' bed. Whenever the baby wakes up, you should get to the baby quickly, he says, since you'll probably have an easier time getting the baby back to sleep if he doesn't scream himself into hysteria first. Here's where having the baby in bed with you is an advantage – you can often soothe, or even breast-feed, your baby without fully coming awake yourself.

To share a bed with your baby safely:

- Keep the bed away from walls and other furniture (to eliminate the danger of the baby getting trapped on the side of the bed).
- Move pillows away from your baby.
- Don't use a wavy waterbed.
- Never sleep with your baby if you have taken any sedative, such as alcohol, over-the-counter cold medications, or narcotics. If the label says that you shouldn't be driving or handling heavy machinery when taking the drug, you shouldn't be sleeping with your baby either.
- For comfort, get the biggest bed you can.
- Use lightweight blankets, not heavy duvets.

## Focal Feedings

This modified 'cry it out' approach is advocated by Joanne Cuthbertson and Susie Schevill, authors of *Helping Your Child Sleep Through the Night*. Their programme varies slightly with the age of the child, but basically it goes like this: Wake up your baby at 11 or 11:30 PM – or just before you are ready to go to bed – and feed him. This will theoretically prevent him from waking up an hour or two later to interrupt your deepest sleep.

If you are breastfeeding, get your partner to go in when your baby wakes up and try to settle him in his crib without picking him up. If he doesn't fall asleep within 10–20 minutes, your partner should pick him up, walk him around - anything to distract him for another hour or so before the next feeding. The idea is to get the baby adjusted to longer periods of sleep between waking. An alternative is to limit the amount of time the baby nurses in the middle of the night (which can be easier for both of you than not feeding her at all). If you are bottle-feeding, dilute the formula so your baby adjusts to receiving fewer calories overnight.

## Scheduled Wakings

In this programme, you try to take control of your baby's night wakings. First note which times your child typically wakes up, then set an alarm clock to wake you up before he does. Then wake him up, feed him and put him back to sleep. After he's used to this, start waking him up later and later, the idea being that he'll eventually forget to wake up on his own.

## Protect the Sleep Schedule

For every programme there seems to be an opposite. Marc Weissbluth, a sleep disorder specialist, advocates never waking your baby – never ever, not even if you're late and absolutely have to leave the house. He believes sleep problems are created when parents interrupt their babies' sleep or allow them to become overtired.

When the baby is very young, Weissbluth advocates putting her to sleep after two hours of being awake, and doing whatever it takes to achieve this. Your baby may cry in protest. Allow the crying to continue from 5–20 minutes, then pick her up and try again. From four months to a year, try making your baby take two naps a day (never in the car or buggy), and then enforce an early bedtime. If the baby cries at bedtime, says Weissbluth, do not go in at all, because 'down is down'.

CHAPTER 5

# Crybabies

When your child is born, she typically greets the world with a wail. You will probably be thrilled to hear that first cry. This will also probably be the last time you will be happy to hear your baby cry. For the next few years you'll be putting a lot of effort into getting your child to stop crying.

## The First Cry

All babies cry. Infants cry an average one to four hours a day. Some infants cry more – a lot more – and some cry less. My next-door neighbour had some of the 'less' babies, and I had some of the 'more'. She spent her evenings sewing; I spent my evenings pacing up and down in front of our house carrying a screaming infant. OK, I was a little jealous of her 'Buddha babies'. Then again, at the age of two her children went through a phase of high-pitched shrieking whenever they wanted something. I was spared that particular challenge, so I suppose it evened out.

## Infant Crying

The first few days after birth your baby may do nothing but sleep and hardly cry at all. Don't congratulate yourself yet. Crying often doesn't really get going until babies are a few weeks old, then usually peaks at six weeks.

A crying baby is trying to tell you something. She may be trying to communicate that she's hungry, or that she ate too much and her stomach hurts. She may be saying that her nappy is wet and it feels yucky, or that she liked that nice warm wet nappy on her and now that you took it off she's cold – and annoyed! She may be saying that she's tired and wants you to rock her to sleep, or that she's bored and wants you to samba dance for her entertainment. She may be saying that she's furious that she can't scoot across the carpet and grab the fire tools – in which case she's going to be crying for the next six or seven months (but will probably crawl early). When you first hold your baby in your arms, you won't understand any of this.

A baby's cry makes both mums' and dads' heartbeats speed up, blood pressure increase and palms sweat. It also heats up the breasts of nursing mothers. Hearing your baby cry may soak your shirt with milk.

Your job is to work out how to understand your infant's language, because crying is a language. The sooner you figure it out, the sooner you'll spend more time listening to your baby coo and babble and less time listening to her shriek.

What you shouldn't be doing, at this point, is trying to teach your baby patience. In fact, the faster you respond to her cries, the better: it's easier to calm a baby who's just started crying, before it escalates into hysteria.

## Translation, Please

While no one has created a baby-cry/English dictionary, the pitch and rhythm of your baby's cry can provide a clue as to where to begin to look for the problem.

- **Tired** – A whimper or somewhat musical cry, it can be somewhat irregular, sometimes accompanied by eye or cheek rubbing. ('This one took us a while to work out,' said Cecily. 'At first we thought he fell asleep because he got so tired from crying. Then we realized that he was crying because he was tired.')
- **Sharp pain** – A shriek, followed by a long silent pause and another shriek. (You'll definitely hear this one when your baby is vaccinated. It can also mean that an air bubble is making his stomach hurt, that he has caught his foot in the bars of the crib, or he is being stabbed by a nappy pin. In my baby Mischa's case, it once meant that he had shoved a toy into his nappy, then sat on it.)
- **Hunger** – Short, rhythmic cries that can sound desperate.
- **Pooing** – Starts out as more than a grunt or a cry, often while eating.
- **Too hot, ill or feverish** – A whiny cry.
- **Anger or frustration** – Your baby may let out screams of outrage when you take a nipple from his mouth or unfasten his nappy, or for no apparent reason.
- **Boredom** – Progresses from gurgling and grumbling to wailing. When you pick up a bored baby, the crying stops instantly.

## Settling a Fretful Baby

Many of the same things that put your baby to sleep when he's tired will soothe him when he's fretful. For home-made white noise, turn on the bathroom fan, tune in static on the radio or switch on the vacuum cleaner or dishwasher.

Doing laundry could kill two birds with one stone. If listening to the washer fill with water doesn't settle her down, sitting in her car seat on top of a vibrating drier (but not being left for even a moment) may. And you'll get something accomplished, too.

A visit to a chiropractor may make some babies – particularly ones who had a rough birth – more comfortable and less tearful.

Don't be afraid to hand him over to someone else. If you're getting tired or frustrated, your baby will know it; a fresh pair of arms may solve the problem. If none are available, and you're reaching your limit, put him down in a safe place and take a short break.

Give yourselves a breath of fresh air – literally. Go outside and get some exercise. Go for a walk or ride an exercise bike with baby in a front pack. The motion may soothe your baby, and the exercise may soothe you. If the weather isn't cooperating, stay inside and dance, holding your baby close (music is optional).

## More Soothing Options

You've picked your baby up, offered to feed him, burped him, changed his nappy, wrapped him in a blanket and taken the blanket off again – and he's still crying. You don't much care why anymore, and he may have forgotten why. You just want him to stop. It's time to try these all-purpose soothers.

## Gearing Up

Some soothing stuff you may want to add to your baby collection:

- **Sling** – Sizes vary, depending on your height. You'll carry your baby more comfortably if you have the right size. Consider two slings, one each for mum and dad.
- **Frontpack** – one of these will keep the baby close, and both your warmth and heartbeat may calm him.
- **Aquarium** – The sound of the filter is soothing, and the fish are distracting to watch.
- **Swing** – The tick-tick of a wind-up swing can be soothing, but this type needs to be rewound fairly often, and rewinding is loud. A battery-operated model may be a better choice. You won't use this for very many months, though, so borrow one if you can.
- **Baby bouncer** – A cloth-covered baby lounge chair that you can bounce with your feet.
- **Music** – Try all kinds. If classical doesn't work, reggae might.

 NEVER shake your baby. It won't make the crying stop and can cause permanent paralysis, seizures, blindness, other brain damage or death. Because babies have large heads and weak neck muscles, shaking a baby causes the brain to bounce about in its skull, tearing blood vessels. If you feel overwhelmed, put the baby in a safe place and walk away.

## Swaddling

In their first few weeks, some babies feel more secure, and are less likely to fuss when wrapped snugly. Swaddling him in a light blanket will contain his flailing arms and legs, which may be startling him, and the security of swaddling will calm him down. (Other babies hate this and will quickly let you know.) If your baby likes to be swaddled, see FIGURE 5-1 to learn how.

1. Position a square blanket like a diamond, and fold the top corner down over itself.
2. Lay your baby on his back on the blanket, the top corner just above his neck. Tuck one arm down and fold the blanket around his body and behind his back.

FIGURE 5-1(a):
Setup

FIGURE 5-1(b):
First wrap

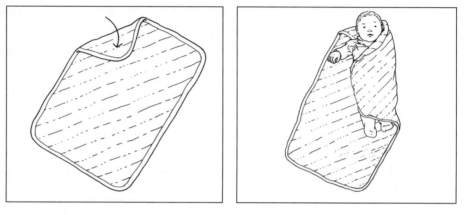

3. Fold up the bottom part of the blanket, folding down any excess that would be covering his face.
4. Tuck the other arm down and fold the remaining corner of the blanket around his body and behind his back.

FIGURE 5-1(c):
Second wrap

FIGURE 5-1(d):
Final wrap

## The Basics

**Keep it moving** – Rock away in your rocking chair in your nursery, or just rock back and forth wherever you are, sitting or standing. Dance slowly around the room. Walk him in the stroller – inside, outside, wherever.

**Sing or chant** – Soft, rhythmic coos may take your baby's mind off whatever is bothering her. You don't need to have a great voice or know the words, just hum something. If you really hate to sing, turn on the vacuum cleaner. It may not sound like much to you, but that annoying hum is music to some babies' ears.

**Change the temperature** – Lisa had no idea her baby would be so sensitive to the heat. 'Our house had been closed up during a heatwave while we were in the hospital. We opened the windows when we got home, but it was still pretty hot. He kept screaming and screaming,' she said.

'We tried everything: nursing, rocking, nappy changes – nothing worked. Finally, as I was walking him up and down the room I noticed that when I walked in front of the fan he stopped crying. I took him out into the cool evening air and walked with him. After that, we put rocking chairs outdoors and really used them.'

If you're not up for going outside, stand in front of the open fridge for a minute or two.

**Change the scenery** – Give your baby something interesting to look at. A plant, a mobile or even a brightly patterned tablecloth will be interesting enough to distract him. Describe what you're looking at, and keep talking softly. He'll start to realize that he can't listen and scream at the same time.

**Go naked** – Babies like skin-to-skin contact – and dad's warm skin works just as well as mum's. Lay the baby down on your chest with your arms wrapped around him. Or, if he likes water, take a warm bath together.

**Be quiet** – Some babies may just need peace and quiet, together without toys, without distractions. Leave him alone. Put him in a comfortable position in his crib or on a blanket on the floor, turn down the lights and keep the noise down.

## Minimize Crying

Babies are meant to be carried. In some cultures, babies are carried as much as 90 per cent of the time, and they don't cry as much as babies in industrialized countries (who spend more of their time alone). In fact, researchers have confirmed that extra carrying results in dramatic reductions in crying. If you don't want your baby to let out more than a whimper once in a while, don't put her down.

This isn't as onerous as it may seem. With such options as frontpacks and slings, and backpacks for older babies, your child can be 'worn' comfortably for hours, leaving your hands free to do other things.

### The Secret of the Sling

Once you work out how to use it, slings will be great for you and your baby. Your baby can hear your heartbeat, see your face and get a ride that is pretty similar to what she felt in the womb. Her weight is evenly distributed on your back, so you're comfortable, and both your hands are free to do what you want. The fact that she can sleep whenever she wants to, you can nurse discreetly, and you're touching her constantly is a benefit for you both.

If you're going to use a sling, wash it many times before you first use it. The fabric will soften, and it will be a lot more comfortable.

Unlike putting a baby in a frontpack, which has a clear place for her head, arms and legs to go, securing a baby in a sling is not intuitive. Your best bet is to get an experienced sling wearer to show you. If that's not possible, refer to the following page for one method. (Note: Slings come in different sizes, based on the height of the wearer. Make sure yours fits.)

I discovered the power of the sling when I had my second child, Nadya. When she started to fuss, I would put her in her sling, go outside, fill my watering can and water the plants on the back patio. By the time I had finished watering all the plants, she was usually asleep.

1. In your left hand, hold the sling by the ring, so the padded area, if there is one, is facing you, and the unpadded area is away from you.
2. Put the sling down on a couch, and smooth it out so that the ring is on the left end and the widest area is on the right. Open up the section that's on the bottom.
3. Place your baby on his back on the opened fabric so his head comes within a hand's width of the ring and his feet are pointed towards the widest end.

FIGURE 5-2(a):
The sling

FIGURE 5-2(b):
Place the baby

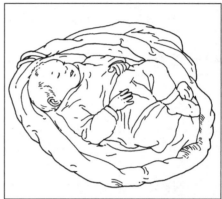

4. Raise your right arm in the air, next to your ear, and dive into the sling with your arm and head. Adjust your position so the pad is on your left shoulder and the ring is near your left armpit.
5. Stand up, supporting your baby until you are sure he is secure.

FIGURE 5-2(c):
'Dive' into the sling

FIGURE 5-2(d):
Final position

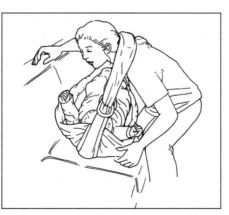
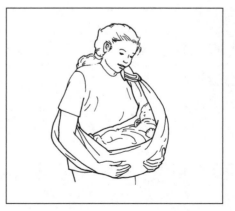

My friend Alissa has embraced baby-wearing. I've seen her only twice in the past year without John, her second child, in her arms or in her sling. And I've never seen John cry – except when he's briefly handed off to someone else.

'I wore Skye until she was three. My husband, Norm, and I still wear John – he's eighteen months now – all the time. When Skye was tiny, we used a frontpack at first, then switched to the sling. People do get put off by slings, because it's hard to work out how to use when the baby is tiny; it does get easier when he gets a little bigger,' explained Alissa. 'My husband uses it more than I do; he loves it.'

## Carrying Power

Here are some suggestions for holds that might calm or soothe your baby. Don't forget that with newborn babies, always support the head and bottom, and keep the baby as snuggled as possible – a baby who suddenly finds herself surrounded by not much but air may be startled.

### Newborn Baby Holds

**Snuggle:** Hold baby facing you, with her head resting on your chest, supporting her head and neck with one hand, and her bottom with the other.

**Football:** Hold baby on one side of your body, supporting the head and neck with your hand and forearm.

FIGURE 5-3:
Snuggle

FIGURE 5-4:
Football

**Knee rest:** With your legs together, put baby face up on thighs, head towards knees, baby's legs bent, holding your hands on either side of his body.

**Shoulder:** Supporting baby's head and neck, place him so that his head is resting on your shoulder. Support his bottom with your other arm.

FIGURE 5-5:
Knee rest

FIGURE 5-6:
Shoulder

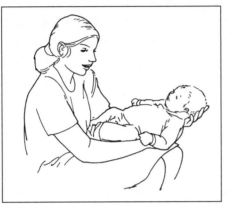

## Older Baby Holds

FIGURE 5-7:
Front carry

FIGURE 5-8:
Hip carry

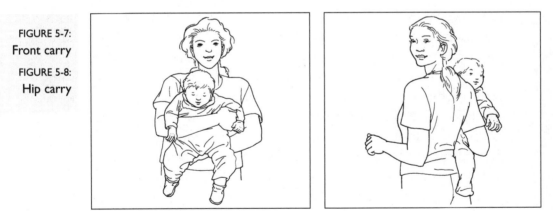

## Could It Be Colic?

Then there are the cries that seem to have no rational cause and don't respond, at least for very long, to soothing. This may mean a baby is just winding down at the end of a long day. But if the crying goes on for hours every day, at roughly the same time, several days a week, then you can feel justified in calling it colic. Some paediatricians use the Rule of Three to diagnose colic: crying for no apparent physical reason for three hours a day, three days a week, for three weeks. By this definition, one out of five babies has colic. (In my case, it was two out of three. It wasn't until I had my third child that I discovered what it was like to have a baby who didn't scream for hours every day of his first three months. You get to finish your dinner, for one thing. You can sometimes talk to your partner or watch TV—it's amazing.)

In spite of trying for more than 50 years, doctors haven't pinpointed the cause of colic. Historically, it is believed to be some kind of abdominal pain (the word 'colic' is derived from *kolon*, which is Greek for large intestine), but even that's not certain.

When your baby won't stop crying, place her in a front carrier and vacuum. The combination of the warmth of your body, the sound of the vacuum and the rhythmic motion as you move back and forth across the floor is almost guaranteed to settle her down.

Colic may originate with an immature digestive system that operates with spasms instead of smooth muscle contractions. Or it may be that certain babies just notice the workings of their digestive system more. Some researchers have suggested that it may be an allergic reaction to something in the mother's diet – in particular, cow's milk. This theory is controversial, as colicky babies don't have any symptoms of the stomach problems associated with such an allergy, like diarrhoea or vomiting. Colic may be the reaction of a baby worn out by trying to make sense of a busy day. Or, perhaps most likely, colic may simply be the ordinary crying of a particularly strong-willed and persistent baby.

## What You Can Do

Because no one really knows what colic is, no one really knows how to fix it. You can try laying the baby face-down with her stomach over a small roll of towels or a warm hot-water bottle. There are several recommended colic positions:

FIGURE 5-9:
Arm drape

FIGURE 5-10:
Colic curl (forward)

FIGURE 5-11:
Colic curl (reverse)

FIGURE 5-12:
Leg pumping

## Colic Remedies

- **Motion:** rocking, riding in a stroller or a car, swinging in a baby swing (or even a car seat swung back and forth), dancing, bicycling her legs.
- **Medication:** For a small amount of babies, persistent crying may have a physical cause. If you are concerned, consult your doctor. Ask your health visitor for advice on dealing with colic.
- **Teas:** Make a tea of fennel, dill, caraway, anise, cumin or coriander seeds by pouring one cup of boiling water over a teaspoon of seeds and steeping for up to 15 minutes. Drink the tea yourself if you're nursing, or feed your baby a spoonful. Catnip and camomile teas are additional alternatives.

- **Dietary changes:** Try eliminating dairy products from your diet if you're nursing, or switch to a soya formula if you're bottle-feeding. The connection between cow's milk and colic is anecdotal at best, but some mothers have had success with this.

## And If That Doesn't Work . . .

In spite of reports that all of these strategies work for some babies some of the time, the odds are that if your baby is truly colicky none of this will help much, and you'll just have to sweat it out.

Colic is tough. Jenny remembers that when her baby first started crying, she'd be calm, soothing. 'Oh my poor sweetie,' she would say, 'let's change your nappy and see if that helps.' By the third hour she'd be shouting, 'WHAT? WHAT IS IT? TELL ME WHAT'S WRONG SO I CAN FIX IT!'

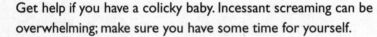
Get help if you have a colicky baby. Incessant screaming can be overwhelming; make sure you have some time for yourself.

The point is to keep trying. (And enlist your partner, your relatives, and your friends to help.) Hold your baby, rock your baby, dance with your baby or just sit and pat him – do anything that seems to help him calm down, even a little. It may seem pointless, but you will know you're trying, and maybe your baby will know, too.

'We would just stay up with my son, with our hands on his chest, while he cried in his car seat,' Lynn said. 'That's all we could do, because he was almost five and a half kilos. That's a heavy load to carry and try to soothe.'

You may be surprised what works. For Esther, the sound of a hairdryer was her saviour. With my first colicky child, it turned out to be dancing to Simon and Garfunkel's first album, *Wednesday Morning 3 AM* (maybe the name was fitting). I thought I had cracked it, but my second child hated Simon and Garfunkel. I didn't get a break from her five nightly hours of screaming until I decided to take her and her big brother to a concert in the park. Before the music started she stopped crying and stared in fascination at all the faces around her. We went out a lot for the rest of that summer.

## The Fourth Month and Beyond

The good news is that parents of colicky babies should see the colic episodes begin to wind down significantly by the beginning of the fourth month (the Chinese consider a hundred days of crying to be normal). The bad news is that older babies can find new reasons for crying.

### Teething Blues

One significant reason for older babies to cry is teething, which typically starts at six or seven months. The gums swell just before a tooth appears, and this can hurt your baby for days. You can help soothe her with things to chew on – teething toys, a leather band, a cold flannel, a frozen bagel (take it away when it starts to soften). You can offer her a bottle of iced water to suck (although sometimes sucking makes the pain worse), or try rubbing her gums. Topical anesthetics, like Bonjela, aren't really worth the hassle of applying to a squirming baby. They work only for a few seconds and taste terrible. (But they can be very useful and soothing for toddlers and older children.)

FIGURE 5-13

The first teeth can appear any time during the first year, and teething continues into the third year. Teeth usually appear in the following order (top teeth above in diagram):

A: Central incisors
B: Lateral incisors
C: Canines
D: First baby molars
E: Second baby molars

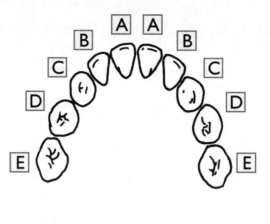

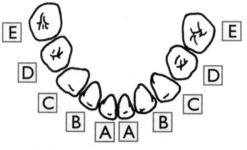

Teething babies fret, cry and wake up more often. And some take it harder than others. 'At one point,' said Moira, 'my baby, Harley, woke up every night around 2 AM and screamed as if he was possessed. His body was rigid, and it seemed as though he was dying in pain. When I mentioned it to the paediatrician, I described it as a fit. He thought it could be related to a brain disorder, like epilepsy, so he ordered an electroencephalogram. But the test showed no abnormal brain activity. It turned out that teething was really the cause of Harley's 'fits'.

## Don't Leave Me!

Separation anxiety is another reason for tears in an older baby. By about eight months your baby is aware enough to notice when you leave, but doesn't understand that you will come back. So he cries – even when you just step out of sight for a moment. When all you want to do is go into the kitchen to get a glass of water, this response can become challenging. (Take heart: it gets better when he learns to crawl and can follow you from room to room.)

CHAPTER 6

# Breast-feeding

Unless you or your baby has a medical condition that precludes breast-feeding – please, please give it a try. If it doesn't work for you, you can phase in bottles at any time. However, recent research indicates that women must breast-feed exclusively during the first three weeks in order for their milk supply to develop fully.

## Breast Is Best

For your baby's first six months of life, eating means milk – breast milk or infant formula. More than 95 per cent of mothers are physically capable of breast-feeding. If you can, you should.

Human milk is designed as the perfect food for infants. It contains elements that researchers are only beginning to discover. Over time, breast milk changes from the colostrum produced in the first few days – which provides babies with antibodies to protect them from the germs they are encountering – to a blend of colostrum and milk, and eventually pure milk. Milk then adjusts in subtle ways as the baby matures. It even changes during the course of a feeding. A nursing baby first receives milk with a lower fat content; as she continues to feed, the fat content of the milk that follows increases. Breast milk is powerful stuff. It can kill bacteria, viruses and intestinal parasites, and can even stop the growth of cancer cells. Breast-fed babies develop fewer allergies and have a lower risk of developing diabetes.

Breast-feeding is natural. Most of you will discover this after the initial awkwardness. Others may find that the first few weeks of figuring out how to breast-feed correctly are a struggle. But it took you at least that long to learn to ride a bicycle, and aren't you glad you did? In the long run, just like that bicycle, breast-feeding will make your life much easier. When your breast-fed baby is hungry, you pick her up, unsnap your nursing bra, and dinner is served. Once you get the hang of it, you'll probably manage to have a free hand – until it's time to unsnap the other side of your bra. You can read, use a telephone, even buy the groceries (online or walking down the aisles) while your baby nurses in a sling.

Breast size, unlike the medical conditions discussed later, is not a factor in breast-feeding success. Women with small breasts are not at a disadvantage. Instead, we may have an advantage – we can easily breast-feed with one hand (or no hands, after a little practice), since we don't have to support the breast, just the baby. And we also may be encouraged to breast-feed longer by the thrill of, for once in our lives, being able to wear clothes that accommodate a cleavage.

'All a woman needs to nurse are milk ducts and nipples – it doesn't matter if she's flat-chested,' said Jessica. 'The only bras that fit my pre-

pregnancy body were sold in the girls' department – and I had so much milk I could have fed twins.'

When your bottle-fed baby is hungry, you have to check the refrigerator or the nappy bag and hope you find a prepared bottle, then warm it up while trying to distract your hungry and increasingly agitated baby. And bottle-feeding is a two-handed operation; you can't do much else while you're holding both the baby and the bottle. Breast milk is easier to digest than formula, so breast-fed babies rarely get diarrhoea or constipation, and (trust me, this is a biggie) their dirty nappies don't stink. There is an odour, but not a particularly bad one. In fact, the stuff looks and kind of smells like Dijon mustard.

Breast-fed infants are less likely to be overweight primary schoolchildren. According to a clinical study, British children who were breast-fed for more than a year were four times less likely to be overweight at school age than children who were breast-fed for two months or less.

There are a host of other reasons to breast-feed – breast-fed babies, statistically, are cleverer and have enhanced cognitive development. Their jaws develop better. It's cheaper. It calms you down when you need it most. You may not get your period back for months and months. And you will probably look back on time spent breast-feeding as one of the most wonderful experiences of your life.

## Doctor Recommended . . .

The Department of Health recommends that:

- Mothers breast-feed for at least the first 12 months of life and as long after as is mutually desired
- Babies breast-feed exclusively for the first six months of life
- Newborn babies nurse whenever they show signs of hunger
- No supplements – including water or formula – should be given to breast-feeding newborn babies unless there is a medical indication

### . . . Mother Approved

In addition to the health and nutrition benefits of breast-feeding, there are the little perks of simplicity and cost savings. Breast-feeding babies are portable; you can take them anywhere for any amount of time without worrying about how long you can keep a bag of bottles cold, or where you can find clean water to mix with powdered formula.

Breast-feeding is environmentally responsible – you don't have packaging, tins or containers to throw out. You also don't have to worry about packing and lugging bottles, teats and paraphernalia with you, or trying to find what you need if you're away from home.

The first two weeks are the hardest, and they don't give you a true picture of what breast-feeding is like. Stick with it through these challenging times before you even think about giving up.

You will also reap the rewards of breast-feeding. It burns off fat better than a gym treadmill, and may protect you from breast cancer. Breast-feeding mellows you when you need it most. Prolactin, the 'mothering hormone', creates a feeling of calmness and well-being.

### You May Need to Feed Your Baby Formula Part- or Full-Time If:

- You need to take a medication that would pass into your breast milk and be dangerous to your baby (make sure you get clear information from your doctor about this).
- You return to work and do not have the opportunity to pump, or are unable to pump enough milk.
- You have had significant breast surgery. Often women with minor breast surgery, like the removal of benign lumps, have no problem breast-feeding. (Breasts that were augmented also function fine, as long as the milk ducts were not cut. Breast reduction surgery typically causes most breast-feeding problems.)
- You have a highly contagious disease, such as HIV or tuberculosis.

## The First Feeding

Your baby has just made his entrance into the world, and, if he's doing well, your partner or a nurse has placed him on your stomach. You can try to nurse him right away if you're up for it, but don't feel like you have to; waiting until you both get your bearings is fine. And even if you're ready, your baby may not be. Don't worry. There really is no rush. You'll both probably have a nap in the hours following the birth. Then you'll both wake up and be ready to tackle this new experience.

When your baby is ready for that very first feeding, go ahead and try it. According to midwife Jean Rasch: 'The baby is born, the baby is hungry, the baby wants to eat, you put the baby on your breast and the baby sucks. It's going to work – why wouldn't it work?'

## On Your Marks

You'll probably want to start with the football hold or cradle hold (see diagram overleaf). Sit up in bed, pull up your hospital gown and settle a pillow on your lap. Make sure your back and elbows are supported; you may need more pillows. Get comfortable. If you have large breasts, tuck a rolled-up flannel or towel under the breast you intend to nurse with, to help support it. Then ask the nurse to hand you the baby.

### Step by Step

Unwrap your baby and pull up his T-shirt, if he's wearing one. You want skin to touch skin. Rotate your baby to face your breast, supporting his head. Then, with the opposite hand, form a C with your thumb and forefinger and cup beneath your breast. Bring the baby close to your breast (don't lean down to the baby, that's a sure path to back pain), and lift up your nipple, making sure not to cover the areola with your hand. Tickle the baby's lips with the tip of your nipple. Wait until he opens really wide and then, bringing his head to your breast, shove your breast in as far as it will go. If you weren't quick enough, your baby may have only the nipple in his mouth. Use your finger to break the suction, take him off the breast, and try again.

Once he's on, check his position. His mouth should be covering at least a third of the areola, and you should hear sucks and swallows. Don't fuss about whether or not his nose seems to be covered by the breast – if he can't breathe, he'll move. Switch sides when you think your baby has drained the first breast; you won't hear swallowing any more, or see his jaws or cheeks working. This may take as few as five minutes or more than 20. Take a burping break when you switch breasts.

## Breast-feeding and Burping Positions

FIGURE 6-1:
Cradle hold

FIGURE 6-2:
Cross-cradle
hold (opposite
arm)

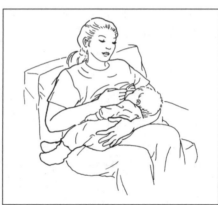

FIGURE 6-3:
Football hold

FIGURE 6-4:
Side-lying hold

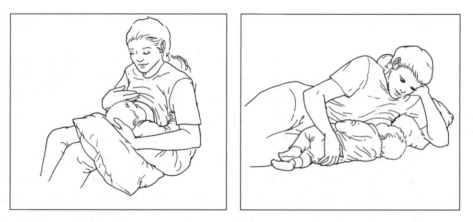

FIGURE 6-5:
Double foot-
ball (twins)

FIGURE 6-6:
Shoulder (high
over shoulder)

FIGURE 6-7:
Lap (sitting
upright)

FIGURE 6-8:
Knees (tummy
down)

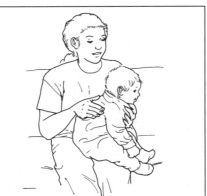 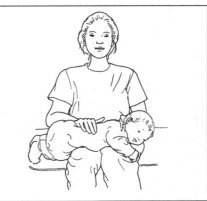

## Get Set

Nurse your baby on both breasts, and do so least eight times a day for at least the first week. Don't worry if you don't seem to have any milk yet; it will take a few days for your milk to come in. Frequent nursing at this point is intended to establish a good milk supply. (Full-term babies can go without anything to eat or drink for days, giving you both plenty of time to learn how to breast-feed. You may have to remind the nurses of this when they suggest giving him a bottle of water or formula.)

At the first feeding, and over the next few days, your baby will be receiving the yellowish fluid called colostrum. Colostrum is full of antibodies and will protect your baby from a host of viruses and infections. It also acts as a laxative that flushes out the meconium – the black, tarry waste accumulated before birth.

Your baby's feeding during these early nursing sessions will trigger the release of prolactin, which relaxes you and stimulates milk production. It will also release another hormone, oxytocin, which causes muscle contractions in the milk lobes, which will force the milk down into the milk ducts, and in the uterus, which will speed your postpartum recovery.

## Keeping It Simple

Breast-feeding is natural, rewarding and good for both you and your baby. However, it is not always easy. While you're both still learning, there are several things you can do to keep things going smoothly:

Find a comfy spot, and get lots of pillows, a big drink of water, milk or watered-down juice, and a book or the TV remote. Put a portable phone within reach, or turn the answering machine on.

- Get comfortable.

- Bring the baby to you, instead of moving yourself to the baby.

- Make sure the baby is latched on correctly. He should have the areola in his mouth, not just the nipple. If it hurts, it's wrong.
- Make sure your baby's head is tipped slightly back and his chin is pressed into your breast. It is the movements of his chin and tongue that draw out the milk.
- Keep your wrist straight. Flexing the wrist that is supporting your baby's head may tip him down into a less efficient nursing position, and the strain on your wrist may cause inflammation and pain.
- Nurse at least 10 to 12 times a day for the first few weeks – that's an average of every two hours.
- Don't watch the clock; let your baby tell you when he's finished.

- Vary your nursing position. The baby will press on your breasts differently depending on how he is positioned.
- Use your finger to break the suction before taking your baby off your nipple. Pulling her off will hurt.
- Have a drink. When your baby is drinking, you should be, too.
- Don't forget to burp your baby. Most babies swallow a little air along with the milk, and this trapped air can cause stomach pains. Try burping when you switch sides and after breast-feeding. But don't worry if your baby doesn't burp; some just don't.

## The Helpful Caregiver

If you're feeling insecure, or aren't sure if the baby is sucking correctly, or you feel uncomfortable in any way, get some expert advice. If you're in the hospital, buzz for the nurse (if you're at home, your midwife will probably still be with you) and ask her to call a lactation consultant, if she's available. If not, ask the nurse to help you position yourself and the baby.

'My baby, Jasper, had difficulty latching on to my left breast,' said Sue. 'I mentioned this to the doctor; he told me to prepare to nurse that side. So, with my husband present, I opened my shirt, undid my nursing bra and positioned Jasper. The doctor came around behind me, put his right arm over my right shoulder, and took my left breast in his hand. My husband and I sat in stunned silence. Then the doctor, very professionally, manipulated my breast into the baby's mouth, showing me how to position my nipple. My husband and I tried to pay attention and not keel over from surprise. And the new position worked perfectly.'

## Breast-feeding Styles

As with sleeping and crying habits, babies' feeding styles vary from baby to baby, as well as individually, depending on what the baby needs at the time. You may find that your baby prefers one of the following styles. (The first five names were coined by researchers at Yale University, USA.)

**Barracuda:** Immediately latches on and feeds vigorously for 10 to 20 minutes.

**Excited Ineffective:** Goes wild at the sight of the breast, grabs it, loses it, and then screams. Try to feed this baby before he's too hungry, and consider getting help with your latch-on technique.

**Procrastinator:** This baby will wait for the real milk, thank you very much, and she'll pass on the colostrum. Don't let this initial lack of interest trick you into giving her a bottle of water or formula; just keep trying to latch her on at regular intervals. Pump between feedings to ensure a sufficient milk supply.

**Gourmet:** This baby will take a delicate taste of the milk, roll it around in his mouth, and perhaps play with the nipple a little before getting down to business. He doesn't like to be rushed.

**Rester:** This baby likes to nurse a few minutes, rest a few minutes, nurse a few minutes more, take a nap and then come back for more. Make sure you find a comfortable seat and surround yourself with books, snacks or whatever you need to keep you happy for what can be a long feeding session.

**Billy Goat:** This baby butts, tugs and pummels you while he feeds. He may be frustrated with your milk flow, which may be too slow or too fast for his taste.

**Regurgitator:** This baby nurses contently for about twenty minutes, then throws half of it back up on your shirt. Then, of course, he's hungry again.

**Barnacle:** This baby latches on tightly and nurses constantly, almost around the clock.

**Sightseer:** This baby doesn't want to miss the passing scene, so her eyes and head wander about while she's nursing. If you have a sightseer, you'll be surprised by just how far your nipples can stretch. Sightseeing tends to emerge in the fourth or fifth month.

**Desserter:** About 20 minutes after a full nursing session, this baby comes back for a couple more sips – for dessert.

## What's in a Name?

Think about what you are going to name the act of breast-feeding because, sooner than you think, your baby will be using that word. (It may sound sweet to ask your infant if he wants 'tittie', but having a toddler scream 'Tittie' in a crowded supermarket is not that sweet.) I ended up going with 'num-nums'. Others have used 'boobie', 'the boob', 'ba', 'snack', 'lunch', 'nurse', 'nurch', 'drink', 'dahda', 'mimi', 'mother's milk' and 'bup'. Some babies have made their own choices – one of my friend's toddlers shouts 'Feed you!' when she wants to nurse; another says 'Off, please'. (At least she's polite.)

# Go!

When your milk comes in – two to four days after birth – replacing the colostrum, you will know it. Your normally squashy breasts will get bigger than you ever imagined possible and may seem as hard as rocks.

'I was huge when my milk first came in,' said Amy. 'I was amazed that my skin could stretch that much.' (This won't last. You may want to put on your skimpiest swimsuit and take a picture, because otherwise you'll never believe you were ever this big.)

Fetch your baby and start nursing, because the longer you wait, the more your breasts will hurt. If your breasts are too hard for your baby to latch on to, put a warm flannel on them for a few minutes or take a shower. You can also massage your milk glands towards your nipple and squeeze out a little milk. If you are still uncomfortable after your baby nurses, put ice on your breasts for a few minutes, or tuck a cold cabbage leaf into your bra. Seriously! Cabbage, possibly because of its sulphur content, draws out the excess fluid to reduce swelling and the cold feels good.

For some women, this transition from colostrum to milk can be rough, but at least it doesn't last long (typically just a day). Said Natasha, 'When my milk came in I went from the size B that I had been during pregnancy to a size E. I sat in the shower and cried all night, it was so painful.'

**How do I know if my baby is eating enough?**

Rest assured if . . .

- He nurses eight to ten times a day.
- He has six to eight wet nappies a day after the first week. (To understand what 'wet nappy' means, pour 60ml/2fl oz of water into a nappy and feel its weight.)
- Your baby's poo resembles Dijon mustard mixed with cottage cheese by the fifth day.
- He seems healthy and alert.
- He gains weight after the first week.
- Your breasts feel full before each feeding, and softer afterwards.

Now when your baby begins to feed, you may feel a tingling or burning sensation a moment before milk begins to leak from your breasts. This is the let-down reflex, caused by the release of oxytocin, which triggers contractions in the muscles surrounding the milk-producing cells to squeeze the milk into the milk ducts. (You don't need to be feeding a baby to trigger this reflex. It can happen during sex, when you see a picture of a baby – the TV advertisement for Pampers always used to get me going – if you hear a baby cry, and sometimes for no apparent reason.) If you don't feel it, you'll still know milk is flowing because your baby will start gulping. (She may also pull away for a moment if the milk is spraying too fast.)

## Gearing Up

The nice thing about breast-feeding is you really don't need anything but your baby and your body. But it's nice to have:

- **Lots of pillows to tuck around you.**
- **A nursing pillow.** There are several types: a wedge that sits on your lap; a wide, partial ring for your waist (great for football holds or nursing twins); and a smaller ring with a back support.

- **A nursing stool.** This is a low stool that lifts your legs just enough to ease the strain on your lower back.
- **Cloth nappies or muslin squares.** Lots of them, to catch messy burps and dribble.
- **Snap-front nursing bras.** They are easier to manage one-handed than those with hooks.
- **An electric pump.** Manual pumps can be hard work.
- **A nursing dress.** You will eventually get sick of untucked shirts, so one official nursing dress is nice to have.
- **A sling.** Great for nursing while on the run.
- **Paperback books.** Nursing is a great time to catch up on your reading, but magazines or hardback books are hard to manage.

## Maintaining Your Milk Supply

You will be best able to breast-feed successfully – barring one of the medical situations previously discussed – if you get plenty of rest, surrender to your baby and are surrounded by people who support you. If friends or relatives are uncomfortable at the sight of you breast-feeding, or keep questioning your ability to feed your baby, avoid them. If your baby wants to nurse every hour or two, let her. Her stomach will eventually get bigger. She'll become strong enough to feed more efficiently, and time between feedings will increase.

## Concerned about Your Milk Supply?

Take more naps, make sure you are eating and drinking enough (a dehydrating airplane trip once destroyed my milk supply for about a day and a half), and let your baby feed more frequently (if she's using a dummy, you might want to take it away for a while).

Moms report success with a number of natural supplements that seem to increase milk production. These may or may not work for you but it probably won't hurt to try one or more. One popular herbal supplement is fenugreek, available in capsules or as a tea; it makes your milk and urine smell like maple syrup. This seems to help some mums (although a few report uncomfortable side effects, including diarrhoea), but don't go overboard. Three cups of tea a day, or two to three capsules taken three times a day, is fine.

Teas made of thistle or borage leaves or fennel seeds have also been reported to help, as has porridge. Eat a bowl in the late afternoon for a boost in the evening, when your milk supply is likely to be at its lowest.

Perhaps one of the oldest and most common prescriptions for boosting milk production is a glass of beer every evening. (Alcohol metabolizes quickly in adults, and therefore one glass is unlikely to affect the baby. But again, don't overdo it.) It seemed to work for me. When we were both nursing, my friend Jodi and I would occasionally share a bottle of beer at 5 PM. I don't know whether it worked because of the extra fluid, the hops, the tranquillizing effect of alcohol, or the fact that we both sat and chatted for an hour or so while we were drinking it.

## What about Bottles?

At some point, be it soon after the baby's birth, or some time later – for example, when your favourite musician is on tour and you really, really want to go to a four-hour concert without worrying about what the loud music is doing to your baby's ears – it may occur to you that it would be nice if your infant had a friendly acquaintance with a bottle. You decide to introduce them.

If you think you'll ever want your baby to take a bottle, get her used to it when she is between four and six weeks old. Too soon could affect your milk supply unless you pump regularly; too much later, and she might not cooperate.

CHAPTER 7

# Hills and Valleys

When you first learned to ride a bicycle, you might have been doing fine for weeks. Then you varied your route and encountered your first hill. Breast-feeding mums hit a few hills in the early weeks. Some, like growth spurts and occasional leaking, are faced by most. Other challenges are rarer, but most can be mastered with determination and perseverance.

## The Growth Spurt

It was almost noon. I had been up with my baby, Alexander, since 5 AM, and hadn't yet taken a shower or got dressed, because 20 minutes after he finished nursing, he wanted to nurse again. Clearly, my baby was starving. I began to wonder if I needed to start supplemental bottles of formula. Actually, I didn't. This was a growth spurt, and, luckily, I had been warned about this (although it took a few hours before I remembered that advice).

Growth spurts are typical at two weeks, six weeks, three months and six months, but can sneak up at any time. Your baby's seemingly endless appetite will let you know when another one has arrived.

I didn't have any formula in the house anyway, and there was no chance of getting to a shop between feedings, or I might have gone for it. Alexander had suddenly jumped up to a higher nutritional requirement level, and he was trying to get my milk supply to meet his changing needs. It was a very rough day and night, but by the next day his hunger and my milk supply were back in synch and feeding times were back to normal.

Expect days when you do nothing but nurse. Console yourself with the fact that you are actually accomplishing a lot – building up your milk supply – and don't go running for a bottle.

## Side Effects

### Leaking

Leaking is most common in the early weeks of nursing, but can happen at any time, particularly when you're used to nursing your baby at fairly regular intervals but get delayed. Leaking can also be triggered by the sound or sight of a baby – any baby – or by sex. My friend Amy even leaked when she heard a dog whine. While leaking itself isn't a problem, the round wet spot on your shirt can be. To avoid or minimize this, wear print shirts, use breast pads or a thick cotton bra, and press against your breasts with your forearm when you begin to feel the tingle that signals a let-down.

## Ouch! (Sore Nipples)

Sore nipples are typically caused by incorrect positioning or improper latch-on. To get over a case of sore nipples, first solve the positioning problem. Then you can:

- Air-dry your nipples after each time you nurse, or use a hairdryer on the cool setting. You can also make sure your nipples get air by cutting the handles off of two tea strainers (preferably plastic) and placing them over your nipples, inside your bra.
- Catch some rays. Find a discreet sunny spot, or use a sun lamp, and sun for your nipples for three minutes several times a day.
- Express a little breast milk and dab it on your nipples. Breast milk has a number of healing properties – take advantage of them.
- Make a cup of tea, then save the tea bag. Used tea bags also have healing properties. Place one (at room temperature) on your sore nipple for a few minutes.
- Soothe them with a lotion. Try a calendula-based nipple cream. Olive oil or gel from an aloe vera leaf (wash your nipple before nursing) are alternatives.
- Apply ice before nursing. Ice acts as a painkiller and helps bring out your nipples for a better latch-on.
- Take a break. Spend a day nursing on only one side to give the other nipple a chance to recover. Either hand-express or pump the resting breast as often as you would nurse.
- Use nipple shields temporarily. These plastic shells fit over your nipples and cushion them while the baby sucks milk through them.
- Make sure your nipples are dry before putting your bra back on.

## Quirks

### Breast Favouritism

Most babies prefer one breast to the other. It may be because of the way you support the baby with your stronger arm, the fact that one breast produces more milk, or that the baby simply prefers to lie on one side instead of the other. To avoid having the less-desired breast go completely into retirement (and make you look lopsided for the duration of breast-feeding), start each feeding with the breast that is out of favor. Your baby may be less likely to be choosy when she's really hungry.

Because Jenny had a flat nipple on her left breast, her baby ended up preferring the right, eventually refusing the left altogether. 'I didn't mind the lopsidedness so much, but when I'd get a sore nipple I did wish I had the other breast available to give the main one a break. If I had to do it again, I'd try harder to keep both breasts in play.'

### Rejection

You can feel pretty insulted when your baby pulls off and cries after nursing for a few minutes and refuses to latch on again. The key to ending rejection is finding the cause. Most common? A flood of milk – too much for your baby to handle. If you suspect that this is the problem, express or pump a little milk before you nurse your baby. If that doesn't sort it out, your baby may have a cold or earache, be teething, hate your new deodorant, or have found that something you ate changed the taste of the milk. It may be as simple as the weather – on a hot day your baby may not want to snuggle against your warm body – or a developmental spurt – your baby suddenly has noticed the world around her. If you can't work out the cause, hang on in there; hunger will eventually prevail.

### Biting

Many breast-feeding mums get bitten at least once when the first teeth come in. They typically let out a yell, startle their baby into tears, then feel horrible about scaring their baby. The baby, however, doesn't try that again for quite a while. If you have a biter, use your finger to take the baby off your breast, say 'No' distinctly and calmly, and hold him off a few seconds before letting him suck again. This usually works after a few bites.

Jenny, though, had a really rough time with biting when she nursed Abbey. It started at about six months. Abbey bit, Jenny shouted, Abbey cried – then began crying every time she'd start to nurse in anticipation of Jenny's yell. It took weeks to overcome that reaction, even though Jenny quickly got her shouting under control and instead quietly said, 'Don't bite mummy, that hurts'. She taught Abbey the sign for 'hurts'. Abbey would bite, then sign 'Hurts'. Finally, a lactation consultant told Jenny not to react at all, and after a week of stifling her reactions, the biting stopped. With Abbey 15 months old, Jenny was able to say, 'Nursing is one of the most enjoyable parts of our day.'

## Speed Bumps

### Clogged Milk Duct

A clogged milk duct is fairly obvious – you feel a small lump in your breast, and it can be painful. (The lump can be anywhere in the ducts, which run all over.) To treat it, put a warm flannel over it for five minutes, then massage the lump gently, pushing the milk down towards your nipple. Then start nursing your baby, making sure the baby is positioned so she faces the clogged duct, and continue massaging. The more you nurse, the faster the clogged duct will drain.

### Breast Infections (Mastitis)

Breast infections are serious. If you have flu-like symptoms, a low fever, red streaks or patches on the breast skin, pain in your breast or a hard lump in your breast, you may have one. Consult your doctor, who may prescribe an antibiotic.

Absolutely do not stop nursing; that will only make the infection worse. Do not delay treatment of a breast infection. Untreated infections can develop abscesses and require surgery. While some mothers may think about trying to cure mastitis without antibiotics – don't. It is not worth getting an abscess, and the antibiotics won't hurt your breast-feeding baby. If you want to use natural remedies, go ahead, but take your antibiotics as well.

## Thrush

Also called a yeast infection, true thrush isn't that common. In fact, thrush today is a popular catch-all diagnosis for any kind of nipple pain. (You may simply have a baby who is a strong feeder and hurts you for a few seconds until he latches on correctly.) See your doctor for a confirmed diagnosis. If you actually do have thrush, you will have cracked nipples that burn the entire time your baby nurses. To control thrush, make sure your nipples and everything that touches them are clean, use a nipple wash (a teaspoon of vinegar in one cup of water), or nystatin cream (a prescription drug) that stops yeast from reproducing.

| COMMON DRUGS: ARE THEY SAFE FOR THE BABY? | |
|---|---|
| **YES:** | **NO:** |
| Paracetamol | Tetracycline |
| Antihistamines (maybe, check with your doctor) | Cyclosporine |
| Ibuprofen | Anticancer drugs |
| Robitussin (guaifenesin) | Amphetamines |
| Antidepressants | Nicotine |
| Decongestants | |
| Most antibiotics | |
| Antacids | |
| Thyroid medications | |
| Insulin | |
| Kaopectate | |
| Vitamins | |
| Vaccines | |

Always tell your doctor or pharmacist that you are breast-feeding before taking any drugs.

## No Let-Down Reflex

Some women have trouble breast-feeding at first because they aren't experiencing a let-down. In fact, some women who give up breast-feeding because they think they don't have enough milk actually have plenty of milk; they just don't have a let-down reflex. Without the let-down reflex the baby gets a trickle of milk, enough to sip, but not to gulp. Stress is the biggest inhibitor of the let-down reflex, so anything that can reduce stress helps, like a warm bath or listening to music. There are also prescription medications that can jump-start a let-down, including Reglan, a prescription anti-nausea drug that can increase milk supply. (I took Reglan briefly after a drug I was given for a migraine headache trashed my milk supply; nursing was quickly brought back on track.) Reglan, however, should not be taken by anyone with a history of depression.

## Too-Fast Milk Flow

Milk coming too fast may make your baby gulp, choke or pull away. You may want to express a little milk first. Try nursing from just one breast at each feeding (you may have to pump the other one between feedings if you're uncomfortable). Try leaning back in a recliner or on pillows while nursing, positioning your baby so the top of her head is above the top of your breast, so she can 'sip} at the milk without it pouring down her throat.

## Flat or Inverted Nipples

If your nipples don't protrude when you're aroused – or in a cold breeze – you may have what breast-feeding books define as inverted nipples. To check, squeeze the areola at the bottom of the nipple and press it toward your chest. If your nipple doesn't protrude, it is flat. Truly inverted nipples can prevent successful breast-feeding, but most will respond to treatment – manually rolling your nipples several times a day, wearing a cup inside your bra that presses the areola and encourages the nipple to protrude, or pumping with a heavy-duty pump.

## Call a Doctor If. . .

- Your baby hasn't had a wet nappy in 24 hours.
- It is the fourth day after the birth and you see no evidence of white-coloured milk (in leakage from your breast or spit from the baby).
- Your baby has no bowel movements on the fourth day after the birth.
- Your baby cannot latch onto a breast.
- Your baby is lethargic and is difficult to wake for feedings.
- Your baby latches on readily but feeds for only a minute or two and then appears to doze off.
- Your baby feeds endlessly, for an hour at a time, and doesn't seem satisfied, then sleeps for less than an hour before crying for another bout of feeding.
- Your breasts are painfully hard and swollen (full and firm is fine, hot and painful is not).
- Your nipples hurt during the entire feeding, not just for a moment at latch-on, and you find yourself dreading feedings or shortening them because of the pain.

# Out to Lunch

People eat in public all the time. They eat in restaurants, they eat in parks, they eat walking down the street. Why shouldn't they?

Well, breast-feeding babies are people. Therefore, breast-feeding babies should eat in public, mainly because there is no reason why they shouldn't. People won't stare – if they do, they, not you, need an attitude adjustment. In fact, you'll get more compliments than criticisms.

Think about it. If you were at the next table in the restaurant, which would you prefer, a quietly breast-feeding baby or a screaming, hysterical baby?

When you're nursing in public, you will set the tone for the reaction of others. If you fumble with your clothes and worry more about flashing a bit of skin than about getting your baby fed, the people around you will feel as awkward as you do. But if you matter-of-factly help your baby latch on, adjust your shirt, then continue your conversation, you won't receive negative attention unless you're surrounded by idiots.

You can also reduce the amount of attention you attract by being proactive. Don't wait until your baby is crying with hunger. Rather, pick your place and time before your baby is starving.

Breast-feeding is a normal part of everyday life – however, you may find people can be quite disapproving of mothers nursing in public. Do not let other people's negative attitudes prevent you from doing what is right for you and your baby.

Slings are great for public breast-feeding. Hitch the sling a little shorter so your baby's head is at your breast, turn the baby towards you, supporting him with one arm, and, after he has latched on, adjust the extra fabric to hide him from view. You can even breast-feed with many styles of frontpacks – lower the frontpack to get the baby's head in the right place, and then keep walking.

No matter where you've nursed, other mothers have nursed in stranger places. I've nursed sitting on a case of beer at a warehouse store (partially sheltered by my shopping cart), which made a fairly comfortable stool; while shopping for groceries at a supermarket; and sitting on a kerb three streets from my house because my screaming baby was flinging herself out of her buggy. There was no other way to get both her and the buggy home.

The other women you meet throughout this book have nursed on the top of a stepladder in an office supply store; while dancing at a wedding; on a couch in a furniture store; on a bed in a department store's furniture area; in a sculpture studio; sitting on the floor in front of a fish tank at an aquarium; on the visitors' platform of an 346m-high tower; while walking through a busy car park; and in award-winning restaurants.

## Dress for Success

While special nursing clothes are available, you don't really need them. You can't wear ordinary dresses and breast-feed easily, but any untucked shirt is fine for nursing (and can often let you nurse more discreetly than special shirts with slits). A nursing bra is good for easy access. Avoid tight bras or underwired bras, which can cause clogged milk ducts.

You'll probably want at least a small supply of breast pads to catch leaks in the early weeks, and then for any time you think you'll be away from your baby for longer than usual. I usually needed a breast pad while I was nursing to catch the let-down from the opposite breast. Change the pads regularly to keep your breasts dry. Disposable pads lined with plastic block air; washable cotton breast pads are better. You can also make your own pads. You can also fold up a cloth handkerchief, or cut circles from cotton nappies or old T-shirts (you'll need several layers).

## The Commitment

During the first few weeks, you're struggling to figure out how to breast-feed and feeling as if all you do all day is feed your baby. This is not the time to decide how long you'll breast-feed. Just keep going without a stop date in mind. Months will pass. You can add bottles – of breast milk or formula – into the routine when you go back to work or need some time to yourself. By the age of six months, your baby will probably start eating cereal and other mushy foods, and you'll be nursing even less.

The current recommendation of the Department of Health is to breast-feed exclusively for the first six months, and then for as long as is mutually desirable. Your baby may wean himself before then – or not. You may want to continue breast-feeding into the second year – or not. You may wean to a bottle or find that your baby does perfectly well with a cup. You may decide to wean because you are pregnant with another child, or choose to continue breast-feeding through your next pregnancy. Once you've made a successful start at breast-feeding, the options for continuing are all yours.

## Guilt-Free Bottle-Feeding

It used to be that nursing mothers were banished to a toilet cubicle, worried about the negative attention they'd attract if they breast-fed in public. Now bottle-feeders are being pushed into the closet.

In spite of her best efforts to breast-feed, Jodi was never able to get a strong let-down to release enough milk to feed her daughter. She turned to bottles, relieved and happy when her child, who had cried inconsolably and lost weight throughout her first month, began thriving on bottles. But she found herself apologizing when she got out a bottle, sometimes putting the baby to her breast for a moment, as if to convince the world that she really was trying to breast-feed. 'I often felt the need to explain that I had tried very hard to breast-feed but had not had enough milk. And, of course, I always knew that the breast-feeders were muttering to themselves that I had just done it wrong.'

Leslie also found herself defensive about bottle-feeding her newborn. 'Everything you read and everything you're told these days leaves you feeling as if you're intentionally putting your baby in harm's way if you're using a bottle and formula. In our case we had no choice, but I always felt as if I had to explain.'

If that sounds like you, don't go running for the nearest toilet cubicle. If you've made the decision to bottle-feed, don't second-guess yourself. There is no going back, so smile at the people who may glare at you and explain if you'd like, but don't beat yourself up about it. Your child will give you plenty of other things to worry about, so save your energy.

CHAPTER 8

# Bring Out the Bottle

Unlike breasts (you've got one pair, and your baby is pretty sure to accept their shape and what comes out of them), bottle-feeding presents you with a number of somewhat confusing options. Whether it's equipment or formulas, prepare yourself for a trial (and error) period as you find out what you and your baby like best.

## Choosing Your Equipment

### Bottles

First, there is the bottle. The three types of bottles (glass, plain plastic, and plastic with disposable liners) come in two sizes: small or large.

That's where simplicity ends. Because each manufacturer tries to distinguish itself from the others, there are hordes of variations within each category. You will find short, fat bottles and long, thin ones. There are ones with a bend in the middle and ones with handles.

The general idea behind all these bottle designs is to make it harder for air to get into the baby. Bottles with liners collapse as the baby sucks. The ones with the bend are intended to be easier to hold at just the right air-bubble-preventing angle, but they're harder to clean. Except for your convenience and your baby's preference, the bottle you choose doesn't matter all that much.

### Teats

What does matter is teat choice. Teats differ in size, shape and flexibility. You want a teat that most resembles the human breast. If you're bottle-feeding from the beginning, your options are open – a generic 'breast' teat is fine. But if you are changing to bottle-feeding from breast-feeding, you need to be more selective. The teat's shape should resemble your nipple's. For example, if you have large breasts with fairly flat nipples, your baby may be uncomfortable drinking from a long teat on a small base. You may need to let your baby test a couple of shapes before you discover what works best. And there are a lot more varieties available than those on the supermarket shelf. Ask your doctor, or check the Web.

When you're shopping for a teat, you'll notice brownish teats and clear teats. The brown teats are typically made of latex; the clear ones are silicon. If you can find a silicon teat in the size and shape you need, I'd recommend it over the rubber one, which has a more noticeable flavour and gets sticky when it gets old. Because the rubber ones are opaque, it's also harder to be certain that they're clean.

FIGURE 8-1:
Standard

FIGURE 8-2:
Orthodontic

FIGURE 8-3:
Wide-based

FIGURE 8-4:
Wide
transition

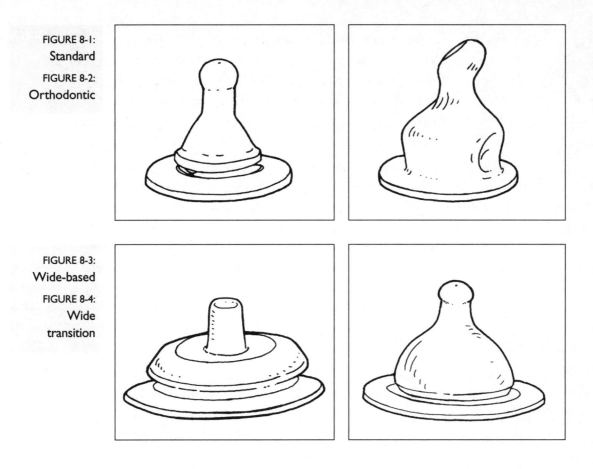

The other key variable is the hole in the teat. Some teats have multiple holes, some have one. Some holes are small, some large. Some are round pricks, and some are cut in an X shape. According to the manufacturers' labels, the small, slow-flow holes are for newborns, while larger, faster-flow teats are intended for older babies. But the manufacturer doesn't always know best – your baby may have a completely different idea.

Because I had a strong let-down, my kids were used to gulping milk, and slow-flowing infant teats made them scream in frustration. I finally tried opening up the hole in one teat with a hot needle so that the milk nearly poured out. When that modification turned my baby into a reasonably willing bottle-feeder, I replaced the newborn teats with the fastest-flowing teats I could find.

**How do you increase a bottle's milk flow?**
For a faster flow, loosen the neck ring. If that doesn't help, you can enlarge the hole of a latex nipple with a needle heated in a flame, or boil the nipple for a few minutes with a small, clean toothpick stuck through the hole.

Even if you have the right teat, you may not always get the right flow of milk, or even the same flow you got the last time. Turn the bottle upside down and shake it a few times. You should see a burst of milk followed by slow, steady drops. You can adjust the flow by loosening or tightening the bottle's ring. You also may find that some supposedly 'fast-flowing' teats are slower than those advertised as 'slow-flowing' – check the flow rates for yourself. Be aware that teat flow may change (typically, but not always, slowing down) with repeated washings.

## Additional Paraphernalia

After you choose your bottles and teats, you'll find that you'll need a few more gadgets to simplify preparing, cleaning and travelling. The good news is that you won't need everything on this list. The better news is that most of the items will be useful long after your baby is beyond bottles.

- Bottles of the right size
- A bottle brush
- A graduated mixing jug for mixing batches of formula
- Bottle warmers (these pads heat up when activated by pinching, and can be recharged by boiling)
- Formula dispenser for travelling (a plastic case with several compartments for pre-measured powdered formula; a two-chambered bottle – one chamber holds powdered formula, one holds water; or you can pre-measure formula into bottle liners, twist-tie them shut, and mix with pre-measured water kept in a separate bottle)
- Sterilizing unit  – very important.

## On the Menu

Next is the question of what goes in the bottle. If you're pumping and have a supply of breast milk, you're all set. If not, you need to select a formula. There are milk-based and soya-based ones. Most formulas are milk-based, but soya-based ones were originally developed for babies who are allergic to cows' milk or had another medical reason for not having milk-based formulas. However, if you suspect this is the case, you should not simply switch to soya. Infant soya formula should only be given on medical advice. There are other formulas available for babies who do not get on well with standard versions – ask your health vistor or doctor for advice. If your baby really can't or won't drink other types of formula, your doctor may recommend a soya-based formula.

> **tips**
>
> Buy more bottles and teats than you think you will need; if you don't have enough, you'll end up scrubbing bottles all day.

You may have to try various formulas if your baby seems to reject one, vomits after most feedings, has constant diarrhoea, or gets a rough, red rash on the face or bottom (no two are exactly alike, so taste-test them yourself). Any formula you use should be iron-fortified. Low-iron formulas, which were once thought to prevent colic and constipation, are not nutritionally complete. (Some organizations are now lobbying for them to be taken off the market.) Any standard formula is fine as long as your baby likes it and seems to digest it well.

Formulas come packaged as a powder, concentrated liquid or ready-to-serve liquid. Powder is the cheapest, most compact and most portable, but can be messy to deal with.

## Fill 'er Up

Young babies are prone to infection, and if you are bottle-feeding, either expressed milk or formula, it is imperative that you keep all the equipment scrupulously clean. After use, scrub all equipment thoroughly in hot soapy water to remove any trace of milk – you will need a bottle brush to get every surface clean, then rinse in cold water. Milk and bottles offer the perfect breeding ground for bacteria, so you must sterilize all feeding equipment for the first six months of your baby's life. Remember that feeding equipment is more than bottles and teats – you will also need to treat scoops, knives used for levelling off the powder, and anything else you use. After your baby is six months old you may use a cup to feed your baby, but if you are still using bottles for any reason, you should continue to sterilize them.

There are three methods of sterilizing:

1.  10 minutes' immersion in a pan of boiling water – you should do this with any new feeding equipment you buy. Make sure everything is immersed in the water and there is no trapped air. This is obviously a cheap method, but is rather inconvenient for anything more than the odd bottle and teat, and if you are predominantly bottle-feeding (either formula or expressed milk) you will get through a lot of bottles! Keep one pan especially for this purpose – never use a pan you have used for cooking. Any bottles not used within three hours will need to be re-sterilized.
2.  Using an electric, steam or microwave sterilizer. These can be expensive to buy but are simple and convenient to use – something you will come to appreciate! Use tongs to remove equipment from the unit, not your hands.
3.  Sterilizing tablets or liquid. After washing the equipment, you soak it in a solution of cold water into which the tablets or liquid have been dissolved. The tablets and liquid are reasonably inexpensive, but making up the solution does take a little time.

Make sure all sterilized equipment is kept covered between uses to keep it sterile. As you will undoubtedly have bottles in various states of storing milk, being cleaned and sterilized, you will probably need to buy about six to cope with the demand.

Wash your hands, wipe off the top of the formula tin, and mix the formula exactly according to the directions (unless you're using a ready-to-use formula, of course). Too little water can cause dehydration, and too much water means your baby won't be getting enough calories.

Pour the formula into the bottle. You probably think the next thing you need to do is to warm the bottle and then shake a few drops on your wrist to check the temperature, just like you've seen on TV. Wrong. In fact, unless your baby is used to a warm bottle, he probably won't care if you serve it to him at room temperature or straight out of the refrigerator, although he may get used to (and come to prefer) the bottle temperature he gets most often. Think of the advantages of a baby that will drink a cold bottle. There's no struggling to warm a bottle while holding a hungry, crying and increasingly agitated baby, and no looking for hot water while on a trip. You can put a bottle in an icebox right next to your bed for nighttime feedings.

Check bottles and teats regularly for signs of wear and tear. If you are in any doubt, throw it out.

If your gourmet child insists on warm bottles, go ahead and do that little wrist ritual – if the milk feels *at all* hot, it is *too* hot. To warm a bottle jug of hot water will do the job. However, you may find having hot water around the baby is a hazard you can do without, in which case you can buy a special bottle warmer.

> **tips**
>
> Take an educated guess at how many bottles your baby will need during a day, and make them in one batch, in the morning, when your baby is not screaming with hunger. You can keep feeds in the fridge for 24 hours.

## Do's and Don'ts of Bottle-feeding

### Do's
Wash your hands thoroughly before touching sterilized equipment
Wash everything thoroughly before sterilizing

Dismantle all equipment completely before washing and sterilizing

Use cooled boiled water to make up a powder feed

Use cooled boiled water to rinse items that have been sterilized with chemicals in cold water

### Don'ts

Don't save leftover milk

Don't keep bottles in the fridge for more than 24 hours

Don't keep made-up feed out of the fridge for more than three hours

Don't use damaged or worn teats

Don't leave sterilized equipment to dry on tea towels, as these may contain bacteria

Remember that you must not put any metal items in a microwave sterilizer

## Dinner Is Served

Settle into a comfortable chair with a nearby table on which to rest the bottle when you stop to reposition the baby. Turn off the phone and try to minimize other distractions. Hold your baby snuggled close, positioning her head in line with the rest of her body. She should be at about a 45-degree angle, so that her ears are higher than her mouth and her head tips back slightly. (If your baby spits up during the feeding, adjust the angle, but don't hold your baby completely flat, as the milk can back up into the Eustachian tube and cause an ear infection.) Pick up the bottle and then, with one finger on the hand holding the bottle, stroke the baby's cheek that is closest to your body. When she turns toward you, brush her lips with the teat, and let her latch on herself; don't stuff it in. Make sure the tip of the teat is in the back of her mouth. Hold the bottle firmly so it resists her suction; otherwise, she'll just be moving the bottle around, instead of getting the milk out.

As she drinks, keep adjusting the angle of the bottle so that the teat is always full of milk, not air. Don't tip the bottle up any more than you have to; the more you tip it up, the faster the flow, and a gulping baby is likely to swallow air. If the flow is too slow, however, your baby may get frustrated and cross, or lose interest and doze off.

When your baby seems to fuss or pull away, stop for a burp, then offer her the bottle again. If she's not interested, don't push her to finish the bottle. And don't become obsessed about how much your baby eats. Nursing mothers don't know how much their babies get, and breast-fed babies do very nicely. The amounts will vary from day to day, so just make sure that your baby is steadily gaining weight.

If your baby doesn't finish a bottle of pumped breast milk, you don't have to throw out the leftovers. Put it back in the refrigerator and bring it out for the next feeding, but, to be safe, don't do this more than twice. Leftover formula breeds bacteria more easily than breast milk, so unfinished amounts should be thrown away.

## Timing the Introduction

If you're breast-feeding and intend to occasionally use a bottle or eventually switch to a bottle full-time, timing is everything. After the third week and before the eighth week. If you start too early, you may permanently reduce your milk supply. If you start too late, your baby may not want to have anything to do with a bottle. After the third week, conduct bottle practice every day. Once your baby has demonstrated that she is willing and able to suck from a bottle's teat, you don't have to continue with daily bottles, but do remind her at least several times a week that milk does, indeed, come in bottles. (Be prepared, though: at six or eight months, she may pull a fast one on you and begin refusing bottles, no matter how successful she's been with them until that point.)

### Another Chance

If you miss this bottle introduction window, your baby may want nothing to do with a bottle. It may not be worth forcing the issue. You can just wait another month or two and then begin teaching your baby to drink from a cup. But if you must wean an unwilling baby to a bottle (because you have to be away from your baby, or must take medication that would be dangerous for your baby, for example), it can be done.

First, make sure that you are holding the baby in a different position than the one in which you breast-feed – facing out, for example – or feed while walking around the room. When you are getting ready to give your baby the bottle, act thrilled and excited, as if you are just about to give her the most delightful treat. Don't act apologetically or appear worried. Expect your baby to reject your first attempts. Give up for a few moments, then try again, still acting as enthusiastically as you possibly can. Remember that even a few swallows taken from a bottle count as a win.

You can start by offering the bottle a few times a day when the baby is hungry, but, if she refuses, take it away. You might try offering a cup, or waiting a little while and then nursing her. If that doesn't work, try completely skipping a feeding, then offer a bottle at the next feeding. The opposite method may work for some babies. That is, introduce the bottle when the baby is not frantically hungry, in hopes that it will be perceived as something fun to play with, and then – what a bonus – the baby gets some milk, too. If this doesn't work, temporarily switch to a dropper or syringe; try anything that will get the milk into the baby's mouth from a source other than the breast.

If you're the nursing mother and are having no success with bottle-feeding, get yourself out of the picture. Let someone else struggle with this early introduction. Typically, most mums turn to the dads, but even better is an experienced bottle-feeder – her confidence will communicate to the baby.

## The Joy of Pumping

Did you ever see a milking machine demonstration at a country fair? Try to picture yourself in the cow's place. 'No way!' you think.

That's what I thought when I had my first baby, anyway. No way am I hooking myself up to one of those electric milking machines. So when my first son was born, I bought a small and much more friendly-looking hand pump. I pumped for a frustrating half-hour a day for weeks, squeezing out a few drops of milk each time, trying to fill a bottle so my husband and I could go out alone for our upcoming anniversary. I did everything I was supposed to. I picked a comfortable chair, used a warm compress and looked at a picture of Alexander, but still only got a few drops. I got a few more when I tried to pump and nurse Alexander simultaneously, but it was a struggle to do that without dropping him. And I eventually gave up and used formula for relief bottles, and then wished I hadn't. The more formula he drank, the less milk I produced, and the more formula he wanted.

**tips**

When you feel oppressed by your role as Snacke Shoppe, remember that this is a short phase. Says Natasha, 'I was sad when my babies stopped nursing. I missed the mandatory sit-and-calm-down time it gave me with my babies.'

When I had my daughter, I got over my milking machine phobia and hired a heavy-duty, double-barrelled electric breast pump, and was able to get up to 125ml (4fl oz) in seven minutes every morning while I watched Richard and Judy. (The bad news was that I started getting a let-down every time Richard and Judy came on.) I pumped every day, and soon had a freezer full of breast milk. In spite of this abundant supply, Nadya never did take to a bottle. So she had breast milk in her sipping cup and on her cereal until she was about a year old. (I even tried it in my coffee one day, having run out of regular milk. If you're ever tempted to do that – don't.)

I pumped again with my third child, wondering if I should bother, given that he wasn't really impressed with bottles either. Then one day, when he was less than three months old, I was flattened by a migraine headache. The emergency room doctor gave me an injection for the pain, reassuring me that the medication was safe for a breast-feeding baby. Safe, maybe. However, the drug was an antihistamine that ruined my milk supply. Over the next three days my husband used up every bag of milk stored in the freezer, while I lay on the couch and moaned.

## Why Bother?

Having a supply of pumped breast milk on hand may be a good idea. Even if you rarely give your baby a bottle, at least he will recognize what's inside it. However, if you don't have a reason to pump – for instance, no plan to go back to work, or to attend an event to which you can't bring your baby - and you don't want to, then don't. Just plan on bringing your baby with you whenever you go out for more than a few hours until he's eating solids. (It's only six months.)

If you do decide to pump, get the most powerful pump you can. Some women with hair-trigger let-downs can use a hand pump or even express milk without a pump, but you'll have a better chance of success with a hospital-grade pump. Portable briefcase-style electric pumps aren't bad, but are not quite as strong as the less-stylish ones.

## Back to Rhythm

Wait until your baby is at least four weeks old and, hopefully, settled into a regular nursing schedule. Pick a time at least an hour after he's nursed and an hour before you expect him to nurse again (or a time when there is something on TV that you like, since it's hard to pump and do much else but sit), and try to pump at the same time every day. If your baby for some reason cuts a feeding short, pump out the remainder. If you experience a let-down during a free moment, grab the pump and take advantage of it.

Use clean pump equipment and bottles (wash with hot soapy water and air-dry on a clean towel or run through the dishwasher). Wash your hands, get comfortable, and then do whatever best produces a let-down. This may be music, silence, looking at a picture of your baby – or Richard and Judy.

When you start to pump, unless your baby has just nursed, you'll probably get very little milk until you get your let-down. Then pump until the milk flow stops. (For the first week don't expect to get much milk; your body has to adjust to producing extra for your pumping sessions.) Start on the minimum setting, and dial the pressure up until you're getting milk. If you're using a single pump, pump for five minutes on each side, alternating for as long as you are producing milk. I suggest you use the adapter that lets you pump both breasts at once – you really don't want a pumping session to last any longer than it has to.

## Storing Breast Milk

Expressed milk can be stored for up to 24 hours in a sterile bottle in the refrigerator, so you can leave enough for the day and night ahead for someone to give your baby. However, if you do want to store more than this, either for future use or because your breasts are overfull, you can freeze freshly expressed milk into a sterile container. If you are freezing milk regularly, leave freshly expressed milk to cool in the fridge before adding it to the milk in the freezer.

Frozen milk will keep for up to three months. To defrost, hold the container under cold running water then gradually increase the temperature of the water until it reaches room temperature. Do not be tempted to thaw the milk in the microwave, because this can create hot spots in the milk which can burn your baby.

CHAPTER 9

# Real Food
# Comes Next

By the time you're finally feeling comfortable about breast- or bottle-feeding, people will start asking you whether your baby has started eating solids (probably sooner than the baby actually should).

## Time for Mush

Currently, the World Health Organization advises that parents wait until their infants are six months old before giving them any food except formula or breast milk. (Several years ago the recommendation was four months.) If you are exclusively breast-feeding, you should definitely wait that long to introduce solids, because even foods as seemingly innocuous as cereal interfere with the efficient absorption of iron from breast milk.

## Reasons for Waiting

By about six months most babies are physically ready to swallow solid foods. The so-called tongue extrusion reflex, in which most things that go into a baby's mouth are quickly pushed out by her tongue, fades away. An older baby's digestive enzymes have matured to the point where she can fairly efficiently break down solid foods. Her intestines have started secreting a protein called immunoglobulin (IgA), which prevents allergens from passing into the bloodstream. It's important to wait for these capacities to develop, because once a breast-fed baby starts solids, she may lose some of her protection against infections and allergies.

I know a lot of first-time mums who gave in to an urge to start solids early. They had those sweet little feeding bibs, tiny white spoons and Peter Rabbit bowls just staring at them from the shelf, and they couldn't wait to play with these new toys. What fun to see your baby light up in surprise at a new taste and lean forward to slurp up every drop! (Or not – like when your baby knocks the spoon onto the floor and then spits all over you.)

## Be Patient

In addition to the health reasons for holding back on solids, there are a few practical ones. Solids will quickly transform the reasonably tolerable smell of a breast-fed baby's poo into foul sludge. Cleaning up spit stains will become challenging. If you've got a trip planned, take it before you enter the solid food stage; a couple of days' worth of baby food can really weigh down your suitcase. (Trust me, you'll be happier if you can postpone the challenge of feeding a baby squirming on your lap in an airplane seat.) At the baby food stage, Lynne's son, Chris, went through nine jars a day. 'Everywhere I went I was packing tons of food,' she said. 'It was easier when he was just nursing.'

The Department of Health and the WHO recommend that once you begin to introduce your baby to solids, you should still give her breast milk or an appropriate formula for the rest of the first year. Cow's milk is not appropriate for babies. Infants over six months who are receiving breast milk as their main drink should be given liquid drops containing vitamins A, C and D – ask your health visitor or clinic. Formula milk for this age group is fortified with vitamins, so no supplement is needed.

**Are any foods off-limits?**
Babies should not be given the following:
Gluten (before six months); salt; cow's milk; shellfish; nuts in any form; honey; eggs (before six months – older babies should only have well-cooked eggs with solid white and yolk).

Alexander let me know in no uncertain terms that he was ready by grabbing the salad and mashed potatoes off my husband's dinner plate and cramming them into his mouth. Lisa's daughter let her know by lunging out of Lisa's arms and grabbing her ice-cream sundae. (Neither of these were exactly the ideal first foods, but we both got the idea.)

So wait the six months – or a little longer – if you can. The window for the introduction of solid food is a lot wider than the window for the introduction of the bottle. Alexander had his first taste of solids at five-and-a-half months (back when the recommended starting time was four months) after we returned from a holiday. My daughter had to wait until after she got over a cold (I didn't want her struggling to swallow with a stuffed nose), again at five-and-a-half months when the experts were suggesting four. My youngest son waited until he was six-and-a-half months, again after a holiday.

Babies can do without solids for as long as eight months without ill effect. Soon after eight months, however, your baby will begin to require the extra nutrients that come with solids. She ought to have a little experience with this new way of eating before that time comes, so starting daily eating practice sometime before eight or nine months is a good idea.

## Your Baby Is Ready for Solids When. . .

- ❑ He's at least six months old (if breast-fed) or at least four months old (if bottle-fed)
- ❑ He imitates a vulture when you're eating, ready to pounce on your food
- ❑ He stops sticking his tongue out when his mouth is touched
- ❑ He sits with support and controls his head well enough to lean forward when he wants more food
- ❑ He's almost ready to sit up on his own
- ❑ He indicates he's full when you are feeding him
- ❑ He drinks more than 1 litre of formula, or breast-feeds six or seven times a day and wants more
- ❑ He's at least twice his birth weight, or at least 6–7kg (13–15lb)

# First 'Real' Food

A better first food than a green salad is rice cereal. Rice is easy to digest, and is unlikely to cause an allergic reaction. Alternatives, particularly if your baby has a tendency to be constipated, are barley and oat cereal. (Avoid wheat at first; wheat allergies are fairly common.)

These foods are the most likely to trigger allergic reactions in some babies. Be alert if you try any of them.

- Citrus fruit, tomatoes, strawberries
- Wheat, corn, soya products
- Egg whites, cow's milk (not suitable for babies under 12 months)
- Shellfish (not suitable for babies under 12 months)
- Peanuts (not suitable for children under three years)

Instant, ready-to-mix rice cereal is widely available, and the standard brands are basically alike. (In spite of my attempts to provide organic food for my babies as often as I could, none of my kids would eat the organic brown rice cereal. No matter how much liquid I added, the stuff had the consistency of glue. Feel free to give it a try, though; maybe your baby will acquire the taste.) To prepare instant rice cereal, mix about two teaspoons of the cereal with breast milk or formula (or, if you're using a cereal that already includes powdered formula, water). Experiment with the texture to see what your baby prefers, but start out with the mixture a bit soupy (but not so thin it runs off the spoon).

You can also make rice cereal from scratch, but the downside is that home-made cereals are not iron-fortified, and at six months your baby is ready for a boost of iron. The cereal-making process can be as simple (rice plus water cooked into a mush) or as elaborate as you choose. One of the mums in my first mother's group fed her baby only cereal made with brown rice, soaked overnight in spring water with strips of seaweed, and cooked fresh every morning in a pressure cooker. (That seemed a little too Earth Mother for me, but her baby slept more than mine did, so she had time for such projects. Instant cereal was about all I could handle at the six-month mark.)

Honey is off-limits during a baby's first year, even in baked foods. Honey contains botulism spores. These are easily disarmed by a mature digestive system, but can cause severe illness, and even death, in babies.

## It's All in the Wrist

For your baby's first supper, pick a time when she's starting to seem hungry, but not frantically so. Forget about assembling the high chair; she won't be ready for that for a few weeks. Instead, put your baby in an infant seat or on the lap of an available adult, making sure she is basically upright, with her head tipped slightly back.

Do not put solid foods in a bottle or an infant feeder unless your doctor has told you to do so (which she will suggest only if your child has one of a very small list of medical conditions). It is easy to overfeed using a feeder, unlike a spoon that your baby can easily push away.

Scoop a tiny bit of cereal on an infant or small teaspoon – or even your own finger – and put it just into the front of your baby's mouth. Don't shove it in; she needs to learn for herself how to get the food off of the spoon and far enough back into her mouth to swallow. Since you're introducing this at a stage when she is mouthing everything in sight, she'll probably open her mouth as soon as the spoon gets close.

Then let your baby do whatever she wants with the cereal. She may try to suck the spoon. If she pushes the cereal out with her tongue, matter-of-factly scoop it off her chin and back into her mouth. (My husband, Eric, having worked as an aide feeding people in a nursing home, was great at this part.) Eventually, she may swallow and then open her mouth for another bite. Once she turns away she's had enough, even if it's only been a few spoonfuls. Respect her appetite, and stop when she's full; don't try to coax in one last bite. Let your baby decide how much she wants to eat. The average baby, once she is eating confidently and has moved to three meals a day, eats the equivalent of one jar of baby food at each meal.

**How much is enough?**
During the first year, solid food is only a supplement – the baby's primary nutrition source remains breast milk or formula. Don't panic if it doesn't seem like your baby is eating all that much.

If she starts to get bored with this new game, wipe her off and put away the spoon and bowl, but bring it out again at around the same time the next day. If she refuses completely – closes her mouth from the beginning, turns away from the spoon or just starts screaming – try again tomorrow. If she refuses several days in a row, give it up for a few weeks and try again; some babies just aren't ready when you think they should be.

## Tricks of the Trade

Be prepared: most feedings don't go all that smoothly. According to Sue, 'It took Jasper an hour to eat a meal, then it took me an hour to clean up.'

Your baby may grab at the spoon – so give her one of her own to hold. (My kids grabbed at every bite that went into their mouths, so I was constantly trading spoons with them.) She may want to squash the cereal with her fingers. Let her – she'll probably suck some off of her fingers as well. She may refuse to open her mouth. Try opening yours wide, and take a bite yourself. (Sometimes I feel like the king's food taster. My youngest won't try any new food until he sees me take a big bite first.)

### Gearing Up

**Stuff to have on hand when your baby is ready to try solid food:**

- Infant feeding spoon or small teaspoon
- Big bibs for baby; apron for you
- Sturdy highchair with safety strap or infant seat
- Topless plastic cups, preferably with handles; unspillable cups
- Food processor or blender
- Flannels
- Disposable self-stick place mats for restaurant tables or highchair trays
- Plastic mat or towel, or dog to catch spills
- Portable clip-on highchair for restaurants or visits

### Don't Stress the Mess

This eating thing is supposed to be fun. If the messiness is driving you crazy, turn up the heat, strip her down to her nappy, and put a towel or shower curtain (for wider coverage) under her chair.

Mums who have the easiest time with the mess that comes with feeding a baby are the ones who own a dog, preferably a big one, with an omnivorous palate. Such dogs position themselves strategically under the highchair and lap up any spills as soon as they hit the ground. These mums say they wouldn't feed a baby without one. The rest of us have made do with newspapers, towels, a plastic mat or just a mop. If the weather's cooperative, feed your baby outside. Hose down the highchair and area under it afterwards. (Remember to remove your baby first.)

## Life after Rice

Stick to rice cereal, once or twice a day, for two weeks or so – or even as long as a month. This food is easy to digest, unlikely to cause allergies, and can be prepared with a thicker consistency as your baby gets more proficient at eating.

**What are signs of a food allergy?**
Any of these symptoms indicate that your baby has reacted unfavourably to the new food you just tried:

- Skin reactions: rashes on the face or trunk, severe nappy rash, hives, eczema
- Digestive problems: vomiting, diarrhoea, wind
- Swollen lips or eyelids
- Fretfulness
- Stuffed nose
- Wheezing, although rare, is a reason to call your doctor immediately. Discuss with your doctor whether the wheezing was caused by the food and whether the food should be eliminated. Other symptoms mean you should just put the food away for a while. Try it again in a couple of months, and odds are it'll be fine.

Slowly introduce other foods to your baby's diet. 'Slowly' is the key word here. Feed your baby a single new food, in tiny portions, for at least three days in a row before moving on to another food, and watch for signs of allergic reaction. (Don't serve a mixed food until you've allergy-tested most of the ingredients first.) It is much easier to allergy-test at the food introduction stage than try to work out what caused an allergy later. It's a good idea to keep a chart of what foods you've introduced, and what reaction, if any, you noticed.

Bananas, potatoes, courgettes, sweet potatoes, carrots and peas all mash easily without special processing and make great baby food. If your baby rejects rice cereal, try oatmeal. Although most mums start their babies on rice, most babies like oatmeal even better.

While there is wide agreement that rice cereal is the perfect first food, there is less agreement about what the second food should be. One theory is that the next few foods should be vegetables, not fruits, so your baby doesn't get the idea that all food is sweet. The other theory holds the opposite, that fruits, because of their sweetness, are more likely to interest your baby, and therefore should be introduced before vegetables.

Both theories made sense to me, so I alternated. Every few weeks I introduced a new type of cereal into the mix as well. My favourite second foods were bananas and avocados (both are easily mashed with a fork), then squash (usually a big hit) and apple sauce. In general, the order doesn't matter that much.

## Top Ten First Foods

10. Peas
9. Sweet potatoes
8. Squash
7. Pears
6. Avocado
5. Bananas
4. Apple sauce
3. Barley cereal
2. Oat cereal
1. Rice cereal

## Baby Food Safety Tips

- Don't feed your baby directly from the jar. Once saliva enzymes from the spoon touch the food, they break down nutrients and speed up spoilage. To avoid waste, spoon a meal's worth of food into a bowl. If you must feed from the jar, throw what's left away.
- Refrigerate unused food immediately.
- Don't keep an open, refrigerated jar of baby food longer than two days – even if it tastes fine to you, bacteria can make your baby ill.
- If you're giving your baby food from a tin, either run the tin opener through the dishwasher, or use one reserved for this purpose (not the one you use to open the dog food).
- Give your baby only pasteurized juices.

## Meat and Dairy

At around eight months you can, if you'd like, give your baby his first taste of meat. But don't panic if those little jars of meat never make it into your baby's mouth. The only one around here who ever ate the baby turkey was our cat. You can try mixing meats with pureed vegetables, or grind up meat from your family's dinner, which at least smells better than the jars of meat. Or you can just wait until your baby is old enough to pick up a bit of chicken and chew it for himself. Meat is not necessary in the first year; your baby is getting all the protein he needs from the formula or breast milk that he is drinking.

Wait until your baby is at least 12 months old before feeding her dairy products. The protein in cow's milk can be difficult to break down.

## Vegetarian Baby

A healthy vegetarian diet that also includes milk and eggs can easily meet all your baby's nutritional needs. A vegetarian diet should include lots of iron-rich foods (dried fruits, beans and fortified cereal), and a daily multivitamin with iron (make sure this is stored out of reach of your baby; iron poisoning can be fatal). It should also incorporate frequent high-calorie snacks and avocados.

Lynne is a vegetarian. 'I'll let my kids decide for themselves when they are old enough to do so,' she said. 'Right now they both eat all kinds of meats and love those disgusting "turkey" drumsticks. I haven't had the guts to look at the ingredients to see what's really in them.'

Meeting all your baby's nutritional needs is less easily accomplished on a vegan (vegetable foods only) diet. Vitamin $B^{12}$ can only be supplied by animal products, and it is also difficult to provide sufficient calcium, vitamin D and riboflavin, which originate largely, but not exclusively, in dairy products. It can be especially difficult for infants on a vegan diet to consume the quantity of food required to provide the necessary amounts of these essential nutrients. Infants also need much higher levels of fat in their diet – necessary for proper brain development – than adults, and a vegan diet is typically a low-fat one.

'Because my husband is a vegetarian, and we are raising our children as vegetarians, people expect us to be able to control our kids' diets better than they can control their kids'. They expect our kids to be on some higher level of nutrition,' said Sue. 'But although we try to get our kids to eat plenty of nuts, beans, tofu, eggs, milk and brown rice, we have fussy eaters just like everyone else. Our kids don't like vegetables; they love pizza, burritos, and peanut butter and jam sandwiches.'

## The Poo Problem

Constipation is not uncommon in the early weeks of introducing solid food. You're giving your baby something a lot harder to digest than breast milk or formula, and the most typical first foods – rice cereal, banana and apple sauce – are binding. Sometimes adding fluids (a bottle or cup of water a day) is enough to solve the problem. You can also feed your baby a little prune juice, or switch from rice cereal and apple sauce to oat cereal and pureed pears.

# Label Literacy

When you're shopping for baby food, you would think a jar of pureed plums would contain, simply, plums. But you can't assume that – check the label. In the past, baby food companies would regularly add sugar and thickeners (like tapioca starch) to their products, reasoning that babies preferred sweeter, smoother foods. (This may be true, but may not be the preference to reinforce.) After a fuss in the press a few years ago, jars of baby foods, at least those designed as first foods, became purer. You should still check the label, however, in particular for foods labelled 'fruit desserts' or 'stage three' foods. If the label says that the product includes fructose or dextrose or maltodextrins, don't be fooled – these are all different forms of sugars. Be on the lookout, too, for corn products, including corn syrup as a sweetener and cornflour as a thickener. These can trigger allergies in a sensitive baby.

Also watch out for and avoid artificial flavours and colours (red #40, yellow #5, etc.). These can cause unpredictable allergic reactions, and there is some unconfirmed evidence implicating them in neurological disorders.

tips

Wash and save your baby-food jars. You can use them to store home-made baby food, a meal-sized portion of food for travel, or a serving's worth of dry baby cereal – add liquid when you're ready. (They also make great insect holders for older kids.)

## All About the Cup

You can begin teaching your baby to drink from a cup at about the same time you start solids.

When your baby starts eating solids, he can also have small amounts of juice, preferably mixed with water. Keep the amount of juice small (less than 125ml/4fl oz a day), or he may fill up on juice and not get the other nutrients that he needs.

You will want him to drink from a cup with a spouted lid: for example, when he's eating finger foods in his highchair and you want him to have a drink available, but don't want him to soak himself if you step away. These cups allow the liquid to flow out in a small stream. The baby still has to control the flow himself, but the liquid pours out fairly slowly if the cup is tipped over.

You'll also want your baby to drink from an unspillable cup. These cups have valves inside their spouts, and don't spill even if shaken. They're great for the buggy, the car, or even wandering around the house. But the experience of drinking from them is closer to that of sucking from a bottle than drinking from a cup, so they shouldn't be your baby's only cups.

It's important to persevere with a cup, as bottles allow liquid too much contact with new teeth and can hinder speech development. They can also become security objects or substitute loveys for your baby, and as such, can be hard to give up.

## Stage Three

At eight or nine or ten months, most babies will be pretty proficient at slurping and swallowing, and you'll be used to the routine. You've allergy-tested a fair number of foods and have quite a long list of things that your baby can and will eat. He's opening his mouth like a little bird whenever he sees the spoon, and you're getting a lot more of his food in his mouth than on his clothes. Daily menus are easy – a few bowls of cereal, a few servings of pureed fruits and vegetables, and you're set.

Then your baby pulls a fast one. 'No more mush!' his pursed lips seem to say as he knocks the spoon out of your hand and pureed carrots spatter across the floor. Your baby is sick of mushy food.

However, he has only a few teeth – and is not nearly ready to handle a knife and fork. You can't expect to pass him the meat and potatoes just yet. (Well, maybe the potatoes.)

## One Lump or Two?

One option is moving to lumpier baby foods. The prepared versions are marked as designated for older babies. If you are making them yourself, don't puree them as long, and leave in some chunks. The change in texture and the more complex tastes of these foods may get your little bird opening his mouth again.

Or not. My kids were used to slurping up baby mush, and food for older babies made them retch and frequently throw up much of their meal. They were ready for something to get their teeth into (or gums, actually; children don't really use their teeth to chew until they are well over two), and the mushy/chewy combination was too confusing for them. What's a parent to do?

## Cereal Strategies

Grab the oat cereal rings. Scatter a few on your baby's tray, and he'll try to pick them up and put them in his mouth. These may entertain him enough for you to slip in a few spoonfuls of mush in between bites.

'Now that Carter is eight months,' said Cecily, 'I need finger food for distraction. While he's busy getting the oat rings near his mouth, I'm ready with the spoonful of squash or pears, waiting for that split second when he opens his mouth and doesn't yet have the ring in place. Otherwise, he cringes when he sees the spoon coming. I think we'll soon be giving up baby food altogether.'

Oat cereal rings are a popular food for nascent self-feeders for a number of reasons. First, they are made of oats, not wheat, so allergies are unlikely to be an issue. Second, they are spit-soluble and quickly soften into easy-to-swallow mush. Unlike peas, they are hard to choke on and more likely to stick to your baby's mouth than to be inhaled. Third, they give your baby great practice at picking things up with his thumb and forefinger. This pincer grasp is a developmental milestone (see Chapter 15) that he is likely to be working on around the same time he becomes interested in self-feeding.

Choking is always a danger. If your baby is under 12 months, do not feed him:

- Whole hot dogs
- Whole grapes
- Raisins, nuts or seeds
- Olives
- Popcorn or potato crisps
- Ice cubes or hard sweets
- Uncooked carrots or apples

Another option is a teething rusk. There are a number of varieties available, or you can make your own. Read the labels; some have a lot more sugar than others. Teething rusks dissolve into mush as your baby gums them. (But don't leave your baby alone with one, since large pieces can break off and pose a choking danger.)

## Finger-Food Buffet

There is no reason your self-feeder should have a boring diet. Provide her with a variety of foods to enhance nutrition and give her important experience with different tastes and textures.

Jessica found out that her daughter craved variety. 'At seven-and-a quarter months, I started putting a few oat cereal rings on Rachel's highchair tray while I was eating dinner. After eight days she ate one, and eventually would eat a few. Over the next six weeks I tried rice crackers, boiled carrot sticks, cooked sweet potato sticks, cheddar cheese sticks, plain yogurt and unsweetened apple sauce, but by nine-and-a-quarter months, she still wasn't big on solids, except for the cheese. (She didn't even eat rice cereal because she wouldn't let me feed her with a spoon, and I didn't see the point of fighting it.) And then we discovered why – we had been boring her. We had lunch at a Mexican restaurant one day, and Rachel decided to try the black beans, loved them, and moved on to the rice and the tortillas, eating more solids in that one meal than she had over the previous six weeks.'

Finger foods must be soft, break down into small pieces, and be easy to swallow. There are a host of fruits that meet those criteria – cantaloupe melons, peaches, pears, plums, kiwi fruits, avocados and even apples, if they are first steamed or poached (slice them, add a spoonful of water, and cook them in the microwave). Just remove any peel and stones, and cut into bite-sized pieces. For vegetables like broccoli, squash and carrots, steam or boil them until reasonably soft.

Pasta makes a great early finger food – pick small shapes, and cook them soft. Serve plain, with tomato sauce, or with pesto. (A garlicky pesto was an early favorite with my babies. Perhaps that shouldn't have been a surprise, as studies have shown that nursing babies prefer breast milk after the mother has eaten garlic.)

**How will I know my baby is ready for finger foods?**
- ❑ He can sit up well in a highchair.
- ❑ He has eaten a number of different pureed foods, including thicker ones.
- ❑ He is beginning to pick up things with his thumb and forefinger, a sign that his motor skills are advancing.

Breakfast foods are also good finger foods at any time of the day. Wholewheatwaffles (purchased frozen and heated in the toaster), pancakes (use a wholewheat mix, make a batch and freeze them; they are easily reheated in the microwave), and French toast (for babies under 12 months, make it with separated egg yolks mixed with formula or breast milk). You can spread any of these with a fruit or vegetable puree to bump up the nutrition.

Whatever you're serving, give your baby only a few pieces at a time, and as soon as throwing the food on the floor becomes more interesting than putting it in her mouth, consider her mealtime finished.

The finger-food stage can start as early as six months, or not until several months later. It depends on your child's personality, for one thing. Babies with strong individual preferences and a lust for independence will move into this stage earlier than more easy-going babies. It also depends on the environment. If you don't mind a mess, your baby probably gets her hands into her cereal regularly, and that has already become her first finger-food experience. If neatness is important to you and you are quick to wipe up spills, your baby may have got the message that she should keep her hands out of the way at mealtime.

By 12 months, your baby will probably do most of her feeding herself. Most of that will be with her fingers – although she may begin to experiment with using a spoon, she probably won't be very successful yet.

## Finger Food Options

For the first couple of months, stick to baby cereals and puréed fruit and vegetables.

### Top Ten Finger Foods: Nine to Twelve Months

10. Ripe peaches
 9. Avocado slices
 8. Small meatballs
 7. Rice
 6. Scrambled egg yolks
 5. Tofu
 4. Toast
 3. Rice cakes
 2. Egg noodles
 1. Well-cooked pasta

## Finger-Food Safety

Since a baby's airway is the size of the tip of his little finger, you should always serve finger foods under constant adult supervision. Only give finger foods to a child who is sitting up – not lying down or walking around. Make sure that all finger foods are soft and cut into small pieces.

## Setting the Pace

Meals at the finger-feeding stage will be messy and may take a long time. Resist the temptation to step in and neatly tuck each bite of food into your baby's mouth. Eating isn't just about nutrition at this point – it's about learning. This is your baby's time to learn to like different tastes and textures; to learn to skilfully get food from the bowl to the mouth, gums or throat; and to learn about when to eat and when to stop.

CHAPTER 10

# Nappy Diaries

You are expected to know all about taking care of a baby, from washing his hair to cutting his toenails. You might think the most important thing to know is how to give your baby a bath. But the bath to nappy-changing ratio suggests that you'll need to know a lot more about changing nappies than how to bathe him.

## The Scoop on Poo

In your baby's first few days, her poo will look like tar – black, sticky and hard to remove. This is meconium, a thick, dark green or black paste that fills a baby's intestines in utero and must be eliminated before she can digest normally. If you're lucky, she'll have eliminated most of the meconium in the hospital. If not, you'll be wiping it off at home. (It's sticky stuff, and may not come off with plain water. Try a little baby oil on a cotton ball.)

In the transitional stage, your baby's bowel movements will turn yellow-green.

If you're breast-feeding, after your milk comes in your baby's poo will resemble seeded, slightly runny Dijon mustard. If you're formula-feeding, it will be more tan-coloured and thicker than peanut butter.

The most amazing thing about this bodily function is how noisy it can be from such a small person. There you are, holding your precious, dozing baby as relatives coo over how sweet she is, when you hear the sound of a volcano erupting. It's definitely a conversation-stopper, and a clue to run, not walk, to the changing table.

Typically, your baby will dirty several nappies a day. But she may have bowel movements as often as ten times a day or as infrequently as once a week. Both are normal. The ten-times-a-day baby does not have diarrhoea, and the once-a-week-baby is not constipated (unless the poo, when it comes, arrives in pellets).

## Nappy Wars

Be forewarned: you will need lots of nappies. I was perfectly happy to let the nurses deal with changing at the hospital. Why not? I thought we'd be doing plenty of nappy changes eventually (some 20,000 and counting, as my third child isn't potty-trained yet). The nurses in the hospital whisked those disposable nappies on and off faster than the eye could see.

Once you get home, however, things aren't quite so simple. First, you have to choose sides – are you going to be on Team Terry (or cloth), or Team Disposable?

There are women who can argue about their nappy choices for hours. One concern is the impact to the environment (disposables become solid waste that must be disposed of in landfill sites; terry nappies use energy and water for laundering, and, if you're using a nappy service, transporting). The other concern is the health of the baby (terry nappies are more natural and you're likely to change them more often; disposables keep baby drier, but leak synthetic pellets when they get overloaded). And there is a middle road – disposable nappies that don't contain chemically synthesized absorbents.

## Team Terry

When I left the hospital with my first child, I thought I was going to play for Team Terry. A stack of cloth nappies, fresh from the nappy service, was waiting for me. I used them exclusively for about a week. During that week I washed countless loads of laundry, because every time Alexander pooed (which was often) it exploded through his clothes. By week two I was using disposables at night. By week three I was using disposables whenever I took my baby out, and by week four I was pretty much using disposables all the time. At week six I cancelled the nappy service. But ever since, I have been impressed by women who used cotton terry nappies exclusively. I feel like I tried to get onto their team but didn't make the grade, so somehow they must be more talented than I am.

I'm not the only terry-nappy dropout. Moira said, 'I was crazy enough to use terry nappiess for six long weeks with my twins. And I often had to change their whole outfits because liquid poo leaked right out of the nappies and nappy covers and got all over their clothes. It created massive piles of laundry. I got my hands chapped from so much washing; they eventually got infected and bled. But, being an environmentalist, I had to give terries a good try.'

Moira and I might have had more success with terries had we started out with disposables for the first month or two, then switched to cotton when the poos become less explosive and less frequent. I might have had more success using cloth with my next two babies, since they had really dirty nappies only once a week instead of five times a day.

It also turns out that, in spite of a changing class at the hospital, I had no real idea of how to make terry nappies work.

## Applied Skills

### Ready-shaped Nappies

Ready-shaped cotton nappies offer a convenient alternative to terry nappies, but are more expensive, as you might expect. However, they are still cheaper than the disposable variety. Ready-shaped napppies are fastened using Velcro or poppers, and some types do not require you to cover them with plastic pants.

### Square Nappies

Fold a standard square nappy into a triangle. Put one point between the legs, and pull the other two points around the side to meet it near the middle of the stomach.

FIGURE 10-1(a):
Set up
FIGURE 10-1(b):
Fasten

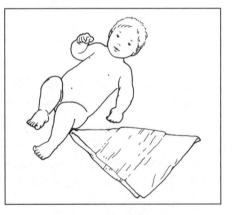

### Changing with a Twist

Alternatively, fold the nappy in thirds but then twist the part that goes between your baby's legs to make it extra thick where it counts. You can fold the nappy down in the front before wrapping it around your baby to give a boy baby extra thickness where he'll need it most.

You can also use two nappies. Place one, folded in half or in thirds, between the baby's legs. Wrap the second nappy on top (using whichever method), and pin only the outside nappy to hold everything in place.

Even better than the prefolded or unfolded square nappies are contoured nappies (not unlike a fitted sheet). These don't need to be folded, as they are designed to fit easily around your baby's bottom. Unfortunately, these aren't often offered by nappy services.

### What's the best way to wash terry nappies?

- Rinse messy nappies in toilet after removing from baby.
- Keep wet nappies in a nappy pail that's about half-full of water; add half a cup of vinegar to water.
- Put nappies in washing machine, run on spin cycle to remove excess water. Reset to full wash cycle in hot water, using mild detergent and bleach.
- Add half a cup of vinegar to final rinse.
- Machine-dry at highest heat, or allow to dry in sun.

Once you've worked out how to fold your baby's nappy, you can fasten it with nappy pins, clips, special tape or a wrap that fastens with snaps or Velcro. If you're using pins, open them up and stick them in a bar of soap before you start changing nappies. Make sure they are out of baby's reach.

## Reasons to Use Terry Nappies

- Terry nappies have a hundred other uses (including peek-a-boo, burping rag, and, sooner than you might think, dust cloth and silver polisher).
- You'll be more attentive to your baby's needs, since you'll have to change her nappy more quickly when she wets it.
- They are less expensive than disposables, so you save money.
- Fewer chemicals are touching your baby's skin.

- There is less waste in the environment, although the chemicals used in frequent laundering may be damaging to the environment..

## Team Disposable

Probably one reason disposables are more popular is that putting them on is more intuitive. Open one up with the tapes or Velcro tags underneath your baby, put her bottom in the middle of the nappy, bring the front of the nappy up between her legs, and fasten the tabs at her waist. However, there are a few tricks to changing with disposables.

### More Tricks

- While your baby still has her umbilical cord, fold the top of the nappy down to turn it into a bikini before fastening.
- Make sure the leg edges are turned out, not folded back under the elastic. This creates a better seal.
- If your disposables fasten with adhesive tapes, make sure not to get anything on the adhesive – lotions, water or powder will ruin their stickiness. If your disposables fasten with Velcro tabs, don't pull the tabs too hard, or they might rip off.
- When you're changing a boy, make sure his penis is pointed down in the centre of the nappy. If you accidentally position his penis up or tucked out of a leg edge, you will end up with a wet lap.
- Even though today's disposables are unlikely to leak until they weigh more than your baby, change them once they get a little squashy. Otherwise, the little pellets of superabsorbent gel burst out of the nappy and are pretty much impossible to get off your baby's skin unless you give him a full bath.

### Reasons to Use Disposable Nappies

- Disposables are required by most daycare centres, and are preferred by babysitters and childminders.

- They're less bulky, so your baby's clothes will fit better.
- You have less financial commitment up front, and you don't need pins or wraps.
- Used nappies go straight out to the rubbish – although they do fill up landfill sites.
- You'll have less laundry to do.
- Fewer changes also mean there is a better chance your baby will sleep all night.

## Changing Strategies

Make sure you have everything you need within reach before you put your baby on the changing table, countertop, bed or floor to change her. Use the dirty nappy to do as much preliminary wiping as you can before you bring out the clean cloths or wipes.

Try not to look disgusted; you want your baby to think getting her nappy changed is fun. Sing, spin a mobile or hold a toy in your mouth – anything to keep your baby entertained and on her back. Clean the baby's bottom with plain water (using an infant flannel, cut-up towel, soft paper towel or cotton balls) for the first month. Save proprietary nappy wipes for later, as they may irritate your baby's skin.

With a girl, make sure you wipe front to back, using a clean section of flannel or piece of cotton each time, to prevent spreading poo to the vagina. Although you shouldn't clean the inside of the lips of the vulva, sometimes it seems as if poo is in every fold, back and front.

With a boy, toss an extra nappy over his penis while you're cleaning him. This reduces the chance of getting a fountain in the face. This isn't a bad precaution when changing a girl, either. Said Julia: 'You normally hear of boys spraying across the room – well, Gabriella could hit the wall over two metres away. And it was such a surprise, I just stood there, with my mouth hanging open, not even trying to cover her up.'

When you've finished, dump whatever is loose from the dirty nappy into the toilet. (This goes for disposable nappies, too. The environmental hazard may not just be the amount of paper in the nappies; another concern is the problems caused by leaching bacteria.)

Dry your baby with a tissues. When you've finished, wash your hands well. Try to let your baby kick for a while so that her bottom is open to the air.

To keep things simple, use distraction as much as possible. Have a special toy she gets only at nappy time (make sure it's light, in case she drops it on herself), sing special songs, make faces.

Changing becomes more challenging as your baby gets more control over her body and can kick away your hands, flip over and, eventually, try to stand up. If she wriggles persistently, move the scene of operation to a washable rug on the floor. (I use washable non-skid bathroom rugs as area rugs in my children's rooms.) You may have to swing a leg over her torso to gently pin her to the floor during some of the wrigglier stages. And once your baby learns to stand up, you may have to learn to change her nappy while she's vertical.

## Gearing Up for Changing

Whether you use terries or disposable, you will spend a lot of time with nappies over the next couple of years. In time, you'll discover what brands and methods work best for you (and your baby). While you're perfecting your technique, there are a few things all changing stations need.

- If you plan on using disposables, keep one bag in the current size, and one bag of the next size up waiting in the wings.
- If you're using terries, you'll need three to four dozen in each size.
- You'll need three to six nappy wraps to go over terry nappies.
- Use flannels for the first month, before switching to nappy wipes.
- Get a nappy pail designed for whichever type of nappies you're using.
- Get a variety of changing pads – one for the changing table, one for travelling, and a larger, waterproof pad for naked time.
- Keep two pad covers in rotation (one on the pad, one in the wash).
- Make sure your changing surface (changing table or empty counter) is tall enough so you don't hurt your back when bending over it.

- Have cream or ointment for nappy rash. You'll need it at some time.
- Invest in a waterproof flannel crib pad, or disposable bed pads. You'll need them now, and they're a good idea to keep for the crib-to-bed transition.
- Above all, keep your sense of humour.

## Changing Tips

Here are some strategies to improve the quality of time spent changing.

- First and foremost, get all your gear together BEFORE you open a dirty nappy. You'll be glad you did.
- If your changing table has a strap, slip your hand between your baby's stomach and the clip before you try to fasten it, to avoid pinching your baby's delicate skin.
- Speed counts – the faster you can get your baby changed and dressed, the happier you're both likely to be.
- Accuracy counts – if the nappy isn't lined up correctly on your baby before you fasten it, it will probably leak.
- Treat nappy rash at the first signs – don't let it get out of hand.
- Put a towel or extra terry nappy under your boy or girl baby, and another one over your boy baby while you're changing. Babies do pee when their nappies are off.
- If you have an active child, give up your changing table and get good at changing your child on the run.
- Stash several special toys in a box near your nappy table, and let your child see these toys only at changing time.
- Always have some nappies on hand that are one size bigger than the nappies that your baby is currently wearing. Nappies seem to become too small overnight, and too-small nappies contribute to nappy blow-outs.
- Use a cloth nappy or a waterproof flannel mattress pad as a changing pad when you're away from home. The sweet little changing pads that come with nappy bags are so waterproof that any accidents run right off the pad onto the couch/chair/lap you're changing him on.

## Nappy Rash

Nappy rash can be as mild as a little redness or as severe as bleeding sores. Some babies seem to get it all the time; others hardly ever. Peak nappy rash times are when babies start to eat solid foods, when they sleep through the night in a dirty nappy, and when they are taking antibiotics. The best way to treat it is to prevent it.

Change nappies frequently (immediately if they're messy). Expose your baby's bottom to air as often as you can and light (even a light bulb helps). When your baby's an infant, this is pretty easy. In a warm room, put him front down on a disposable absorbent pad or use a waterproof crib pad with a terry nappy on top of it. Once your baby is mobile, it is less likely he'll stay put. If it's summer, let him run around bare-bottomed outside. If it's winter, you might consider heating up your bathroom and giving him a little extra naked time after his bath. This also has the advantage of providing valuable 'tummy time', because your baby sleeps on his back.

**Cure nappy rash in the same way you prevent it – with dryness and air.**

What you don't have to do to prevent nappy rash is lather on ointment with every nappy change.

If you notice a little redness – the beginnings of nappy rash – start to treat it immediately. Don't just hope it will go away on it's own; it's likely to get worse, becoming a lot more uncomfortable for your baby and a lot harder for you to treat. Also understand that, left untreated, a simple case of nappy rash can become a yeast infection, which is a lot harder to get rid of than ordinary nappy rash. (A yeast infection typically comes on quickly and intensely, characterized by a bright red rash around the nappy area, with small red pimples here and there in the surrounding areas.)

'It's really hard to make nappy rash go away unless you just take off your baby's nappy and let him pee all over the floor,' said Laura.

If that sounds too messy for you, and it's warm outside, let him roll around on a towel on the grass. Or, put a terry nappy down in your buggy, sit your baby on top of it, and go for a long walk.

## Rash Remedies

Ointments come into play when your baby has nappy rash and can't be naked. These are typically zinc and castor oil creams – check that your baby is not sensitive to wipes or creams.

If you suspect a yeast infection, ask your doctor for advice; and only use nappy rash creams or wipes for as long as they are needed to clear up the rash.

Baby powder isn't much help in protecting against or curing nappy rash, and talc-based powders can be particularly dangerous when inhaled. Cornflour powders gather in skin folds and can encourage the growth of yeast. When carefully applied, powder is not necessarily bad, but it doesn't serve any great purpose, either.

If you're using disposable nappies, consider peeling off the outside plastic cover and fastening a terry nappy around it. That combination will prevent leaks while allowing air to get through.

If your baby has graduated to wipes, you should go back to using plain water to clean your baby's bottom while he's rashy. Nappy wipes may make the rash worse.

## Intimate Care

The first time I changed a nappy and saw a spot of blood, I panicked. However, in the early days red spots are not a concern. They can come from urates, which are normal crystals in a baby's urine that turn to a salmon colour on the nappy. In girls, spots within the first week home may also be a small amount of bloody vaginal discharge caused by the mother's hormones.

## Penis Care

Don't retract the foreskin for cleaning; if you force it, you could cause bleeding and scarring. Normal bathing will keep him clean. If your son has been circumcized, for religious or health reasons, your doctor or health visitor can advise you.

## Bellybutton Care

Your baby's bellybutton needs special attention until the cord dries up and falls off (this is usually around four to five days, but can be up to two weeks), because this area can get infected. To prevent infection, keep his bellybutton dry and clean, and expose it to air as much as possible.

That doesn't necessarily mean you shouldn't immerse your baby in water until the cord is gone, only that you shouldn't cover the cord area until it is completely dry – use a hairdryer if you need to. (Paediatricians have different opinions about this; check with yours.) If you see any signs of redness or pus, however, don't immerse her and call your paediatrician.

You'll probably be told to swab around the base of the cord with a cotton ball dipped in surgical spirit several times a day. This has a dual purpose – the spirit both kills bacteria and dries out the cord. (Although recent studies have shown that water may work just as well, your doctor will probably recommend surgical spirit.) Alternatives are witch hazel extract, an astringent; compresses soaked with a tea made from dried comfrey leaves, which soothe and may speed up healing; and powdered rosemary leaves, dusted on the cord stump to prevent infection.

You may see a few drops of blood as the cord detaches. This is normal, as is a little yellow discharge. Redness on the skin around the bellybutton or oozing pus are not normal, and if you see either, call your doctor immediately.

CHAPTER 11

# Baths and Beyond

nfants don't get all that dirty, so one bath a week is plenty until she's eating solid foods and crawling in the dirt. Just be sure to wash her face, hands, neck and nappy area daily. If your baby likes her bath, you *can* bathe her every day, as long as you limit her bath to no more than ten minutes.

## Bath Time

Who are we kidding? The first bath is a major photo opportunity, and you'll probably want to do it sooner rather than later. There are a couple of approaches, and you'll discover, with practice, which method works best for you and your baby.

### What You Need

The first few baths are relatively simple – you're just concentrating on keeping your baby warm, making him feel secure and getting him clean. As he grows, of course, toys and boats and ducks will take more room in the tub than he does. In the meantime, stock up on some simple, yet highly recommended, bath aids!

- Cotton balls (for cleaning eyes and ears)
- Plastic cup or spray bottle
- Soft brush
- Baby flannels (lots, for washing, warmth and play)
- Several towels
- Fluffy towels or baby to lie on
- Baby soap or no-tears shampoo (the two are pretty well interchangeable)
- Baby bathtub or clean sink
- Foam pad to kneel on when you're bathing your baby in an adult tub (special pads are available for this purpose, or you can use kneelers designed for gardening)
- Non-skid mat (for use in an adult tub)
- Foam tap cover or flannel or small towel (for an adult tub)

### The Sponge Bath

If you decide that your baby's first bath should be a sponge bath, give yourself plenty of time to work out exactly where you're going to conduct this operation. You don't want to be running around the house with a naked baby, trying to decide where to bathe him. Your best choice is a counter next to the sink, if your counter is big enough. This has several advantages. Cleaning up will be easy since it's waterproof, it's high enough to keep you from wrecking your back, it provides a ready source of warm water, and it makes it easier to rinse your baby's hair.

Babies are slippery when wet! They are less likely to slip when held by a big hand, so if bigger hands than yours are available, this might be the time to call them into service.

You'll need something soft to put your baby on. A thick, folded bath towel is fine. If you have a baby bathtub that came with a thick contoured sponge, save the tub for later, but place the sponge on the counter.

Make sure you have everything that you need within reach. You'll need several towels. In addition to the one on which your baby's lying, you'll need one to keep parts of him warm while you're bathing other parts, and another one to dry him. You'll also need:

- At least two flannels (you don't want to wipe a spot of milk from his face with the same flannel you just used to wipe his backside)
- Cotton balls, or another clean flannel, for his eyes
- Baby soap
- A clean nappy
- Clean clothes
- Barrier cream
- Plastic cup
- Bowl of cooled boiled water

Strip the baby down to his nappy, and lay him on the towel. Cover him with the other towel; you'll uncover only the piece of baby you're washing at the moment.

Wipe inside the corners of his eyes, from inside out, using a clean cotton ball or a different corner of the flannel for each eye. You can use cotton balls to wipe his ear folds as well. But don't try to wash inside the ear canal, even if you see wax. The wax protects the inner ear.

Pay special attention to all the creases around his neck, which may be filled with gunk. With a newborn, this gunk is likely to be skin cells sloughing off; with an older baby, the gunk is likely to be dried food. Then move on to washing his limbs and the front of his torso.

To wash his hair, wet it with the flannel, add a dab of soap, and gently massage the entire scalp, including the soft spots. You don't really need a special baby shampoo; liquid baby bath is an all-purpose cleaner at this stage. Then hold your baby so his head, supported by one hand, is tipped slightly back over the sink. Using the plastic cup, pour warm water back over his head, avoiding his eyes. If some soap does get into his eyes, wipe them with plain, warm water; he'll open his eyes once the soap is gone.

Next, take off his nappy and wash his bottom and genitals. (If you're bathing a girl, remember to always wash from front to back.) Finish by sitting him up, leaning him forward on your hand as if you're going to burp him, and wash his back. Check to make sure all the soap is rinsed off, and dry him with a clean towel, again paying particular attention to the creases in his neck.

## Into the Tiny Tub

When you're ready to get your baby off the counter and into the tub, you don't need an official baby bathtub. You can bathe your baby in a clean dishpan or even the sink itself. When I had my first son, my hospital supplies (the spray bottle, soap and shampoo, and a couple of ice packs) were handed to me in a tiny pink plastic basin, about two-thirds the size of a normal washing-up bowl. The nurse advised me to save the basin, as it made a perfect baby bath. It looked impossibly small, but it worked perfectly and meant one less large, primary-coloured plastic object cluttering up my house.

Do not ever, even for a second, leave a baby alone in a bath.

Whatever type of tub you choose, think of your back when you're positioning it. Having the tub in the sink or up on the counter will be easier to manage than crouching over it on the floor. When I had two kids to bathe, I discovered that the baby tub a friend had lent to me hooked solidly across our big tub. If yours doesn't fit well, and you're trying to bathe two kids at once, put the baby tub with its stopper unplugged right inside the big tub – there should be room left for your older child.

Gather up all your supplies while your baby is still dressed. Fill the bath with only 50–75mm (3–4in) of lukewarm water; test the temperature on the inside of your wrist or elbow. The idea here is that most of your baby's body and all of her face should be well above the water line. You'll keep her warm by layering extra flannels over her stomach and pouring warm water on them regularly. (This is a great job to give to a sibling.)

## Bath-Time Tips

Try these strategies for improving bath-time efficiency, safety and fun:

- Turn your hot water heater to a low setting (about 50°C/120°F) to avoid dangerous burns.
- Put liquid baby soap into a clean pump dispenser for one-handed use.
- Save the spray bottle the hospital gave you for cleaning your perineum and use it to rinse your baby's hair.
- Bring on the flannels – the more the merrier. In addition to the one you're using for washing, spread a few others across your baby to keep him warm. If you have another child, give her a flannel to soak with water and drip onto the baby's tummy. You may be rewarded with tandem giggles.
- Pat your baby dry. Don't rub; rubbing can irritate delicate baby skin.
- Heat the towels in the dryer – your baby will love the snuggly warmth.
- The kitchen sink makes a great place for a baby bath, if you have a spray hose and tap that can be turned out of the way, and all the the dishes have been done.
- Save your back. Put the baby bathtub on a counter.
- Make your baby comfortable in the baby bath or sink and reduce the chance of his sliding around. Put a folded towel or special-purpose bath sponge on the bottom before you put your baby in the water.

- When your baby is ready to graduate from the infant tub to the big tub, start out by placing the infant tub inside the big tub for a few baths to get him used to the transition.
- Bathe with your baby. It's a lot easier on your back than leaning over the tub, and you're bound to get wet anyway. (If you have a hard time finding enough time for your own bath in a normal day, this idea is for you.)
- Get a spray hose that attaches to the bath tap or taps; you can use it to rinse your baby with clean water, and it makes hair-washing much easier.

## Graduating to the Big Tub

Your baby is ready to graduate to an adult bathtub once he can sit steadily without support (usually some time after six months).

You'll find that baby stores sell bath seats or rings for this stage. These will give your baby extra support, but probably aren't worth a trip to buy them. Your baby won't use a bath ring for long; as soon as he starts crawling, he'll want to explore the tub. A bath ring or seat may give you a false sense of confidence. Even when your baby is in a bath ring or seat, you need to stay within grabbing distance – these devices don't keep a baby from tipping over and slipping under the water.

Your best bet may be to get in the tub with him and support him between your legs. This is a two-person job. One person gets in the tub first, then the other one hands off the baby. (Reverse the procedure on the way out.)

Since a towel or sponge on the bottom of a regular tub will slide all over, get a non-skid mat if your baby seems not to like sitting on the bathtub's hard surface. This will be softer to sit on, as well as safer.

## Bath Toys

Your baby will be interested in bath toys at this point, but keep them simple – a few things that float and a cup that pours water are plenty.

- Nylon bath puff, flannel (use the flannel to wrap up tub toys for baby to unwrap)
- Floating plastic book
- Spray bottle
- Rubber duck, boats, bath puppet
- Full bottles of shampoo, conditioner and anything else that's not a toy
- Siblings

## Cradle Cap

When you're washing your baby's head, you may see thick, yellow scales. This is cradle cap, and, although it looks pretty yucky, it's benign. You could let it go away on its own, or try this instead. Rub olive oil onto the scalp, let it soak for a few hours, then scrub the cradle cap away with a baby hair brush, baby toothbrush or nailbrush, followed by a mild baby shampoo to get the oil out. You'll have to scrub harder than you think. Don't worry, you won't hurt your baby. I tried for weeks to softly brush off my son's case of cradle cap (since he was a bald baby, it looked particularly disgusting) with no success. Then my much more experienced babysitter took brush in hand and scrubbed it away – without a whimper from Alex.

## Trimming Nails

Of all the baby-care tasks, nothing seems to panic parents more than the idea of cutting their baby's nails.

'I drew blood once, and it was horrible,' said Anna. 'I think that I cried longer than Bobby did. Sometimes now I can only bring myself to cut two nails at a time – it takes all week to do them all.'

'The first time I tried to cut Gabriella's nails, I cut the tip of her finger and it bled and bled.' Julia said. 'The next time I let my surgeon father-in-law do it, and since then, I just save it until he comes to visit.'

My daughter was born with talons. During her first day of life I kept staring at them, knowing I really needed to cut them but wondering how I could do it without cutting off her tiny fingers. The pediatrician came in the next day to check her. She borrowed my manicure scissors and trimmed Nadya's nails in about 30 seconds – experience does count.

Some parents swear by biting off their baby's nails. This isn't hard to do, because the nails are so soft. But don]t do this, as you risk tearing the nail down into the skin. I could never bring myself to do this. I don't bite my own nails, and it seemed really strange to consider biting my baby's.

You could avoid the whole issue and put your baby into cotton mittens, but odds are your baby isn't going to like wearing those for long. And frankly, nail-cutting is just more traumatic for parents than it is for babies. My husband still won't cut any of our kids' nails, and my oldest son is nine. If you do accidentally nick your child, it really won't hurt all that much and will heal quickly.

## Clippers or Scissors?

Seems to me that parents are evenly divided between clippers and scissors. Clippers seem safer than scissors, but can actually cause more damage. The best guide is probably what you're more comfortable using on your own nails – as I said, experience counts. And you may discover, as I did, that your own manicure scissors are actually less likely to draw blood than blunt-tipped infant nail scissors. The blunt tip does keep you from stabbing your baby, but that isn't so much of a risk. The bigger problem is that the blades of baby scissors tend to be a little thicker and difficult to slip easily under your baby's nails, making it more likely that you'll pinch the soft skin.

## Trim Time

Wait until your baby is in a deep sleep when you're learning to trim nails. This means her arms and legs flop when lifted, and her hand is resting open, not in a fist. Hold the scissors or clippers in one hand; with the other, pull the tip of her finger down away from the nail. You should now have better access to the nail, so go ahead and cut. Cut straight across. If you're worried about sharp corners, you can gently file them later. If you do cut your baby, press on the cut and the bleeding will quickly stop. You can also dab on antiseptic first-aid cream.

'I cut off half of my daughter's thumb with nail clippers the night after we got home from the hospital – or so it seemed at the time,' Hilary said. 'She didn't wake up, and recovered within a few days, but I was traumatized and haven't been able to use scissors or clippers since.'

You will get better with practice – and you will get plenty of practice. Your infant's fingernails may need to be trimmed several times a week. Toenails grow at a slower rate, and should be cut every couple of weeks.

## Beginning Tooth Care

Come now, you're thinking, she can't really want me to think about brushing teeth already – my baby won't have any teeth for ages.

Well, yes, actually, you should start thinking about brushing teeth now. You need to get your baby used to having her gums cleaned before her teeth come in. The first few times you try it, she's likely to bite you, and you're much better off getting those bites over with before they can draw blood. Still, it's not likely to be fun. Says Leda, 'Brushing teeth is second only to hair-washing in terms of difficulty. It is one of the most stressful times of the morning, and we do not even attempt to do it at night.'

**What can I do now to make brushing teeth fun for my baby?**
Brushing your baby's 'teeth' is a good habit to start now, not only for healthy gums and developing teeth, but to establish it in his routine. Here are some tips to make brushing teeth fun.

- Babies love to imitate. Brush your teeth in front of your baby before you try to brush his teeth.
- Name your baby's teeth and sing to them while you brush.
- Look for something silly hiding behind your baby's teeth.

Once your baby has two or more teeth, wipe the teeth and gums each evening with a clean wet handkerchief wrapped around your finger. There's no need to use toothpaste at this stage. When you do introduce toothpaste, make sure that it does not contain sugar – some children's brands do.

## Sunshine and Naked Time

A number of infant care problems can be avoided by letting your baby lie around naked. If he can spend some of his 'naked time' in the sun – outside, or in a patch of sun from a window – so much the better. Sunbaths help prevent nappy rash, heal the umbilical cord and prevent newborn jaundice by breaking down the bilirubin in the blood. We're not talking about going for the fake tan look, of course – just five minutes of sun a day, in the early morning or late afternoon, are plenty (avoid the middle of the day and early afternoon, when the sun's rays are at their strongest). And make sure your baby is facing away from the sun, or that his eyes are covered.

CHAPTER 12

# In Sickness and Health

He's ill!!! Do you call the doctor? Run to accident and emergency? Give him medicine? Or just put him back to sleep? You're the casualty nurse and you have to work it out – which isn't easy, because he's still screaming. Here are some baby-health basics.

# Infant Alert: The First Month

## Time to Call the Doctor

You're more likely to need to call the doctor while your baby is newborn. Symptoms that are not worrying in an older baby can indicate real trouble during a baby's first month.

- **Jaundice.** Many babies develop a yellow tinge to their skin colour after birth. This is caused by increased amounts of a pigment called bilirubin, which is produced by the normal breakdown of red blood cells. Normal jaundice occurs in more than 50 per cent of babies, appearing at day two or three and disappearing in a week or two; it's usually harmless.

  So-called breast-milk jaundice (originally thought to be caused by an enzyme in mother's milk) looks the same, but usually appears between days four and seven and can last three to ten weeks. You may find it helpful to nurse more frequently, every one-and-a-half to two-and-a-half hours during the day, and at least every four hours at night. Frequent feeding may seem counter-intuitive, but it does mean frequent pooing, and that helps cleanse bilirubin from the body.

  Call your doctor immediately if your jaundiced baby becomes dehydrated or feverish. Call your doctor during her regular office hours if your baby looks deep yellow or orange, has fewer than three movements a day, or still looks yellow after she is fourteen days old.

- **Fever.** Call the doctor if your baby's temperature is over 37.2°C (99.0°F) axillary (under the arm). A fever in the first two months may be a sign of a serious infection, and an infection at this age can quickly overwhelm the developing immune system. Your baby may be hospitalized and treated with antibiotics.

- **Diarrhoea.** Diarrhoea in newborns can quickly lead to dehydration. While babies normally have many bowel movements a day, and they are typically runny, if it looks more like water than like mustard it is diarrhoea. If you suspect diarrhoea, and your baby is pooing more often than she is eating, call the doctor.

- **Vomiting.** Projectile vomiting (vomit that shoots out of the mouth instead of dribbling down the chin) may mean your baby has an obstruction in the valve between the stomach and small intestine. Call your doctor immediately.

    Vomiting after more than three feedings in a row may cause dehydration. Call your doctor if your baby doesn't pee in eight hours.

- **Floppiness.** While a newborn doesn't have a lot of muscle control, he typically kicks and squirms and waves his arms around. If he feels floppy all over or seems to lose muscle tone, he may have an infection, so call the doctor.

- **Shakes.** A quivering chin is sweet, but if your baby seems to quiver all over, your doctor needs to find out why.

Before you call the doctor, make sure you have the following information to hand:

- Your doctor's name
- Your baby's temperature (even if it's normal)
- A list of his symptoms, starting with the ones that concern you most, and an estimate of their duration
- Information about what you've done to address his symptoms
- The phone number of a pharmacy that is open and convenient
- Your child's weight at his last check-up (in case your doctor wants to check on the dosage of a medication)

## Older Baby Symptoms

If your baby is more than a month old, you don't need to be quite so quick to phone the doctor. But you should call if your baby:

- Is under six months old and has a fever higher than 38.3°C (101°F)
- Is over six months old has a fever higher than 39.4°C (103°F)
- Has a fever for more than two days

- Has a fever and a stiff neck, symptoms of meningitis (Check for this by holding a toy level with her face and then moving it toward the ground. If she can't follow its path by bringing her chin down to her chest, she may have a stiff neck.)
- Is too sleepy (You may be relieved if your baby suddenly starts to sleep all day and night, but a big jump in sleepiness is not normal and may indicate an infection.)
- Cries excessively
- Vomits persistently (after every feeding within 12 hours), or if the vomit contains blood
- Seems dehydrated (If your baby seems to be peeing a lot less than usual – you're changing fewer nappies – there is a problem.)
- Has trouble breathing (the skin between her ribs may be sucked in with each breath), or breathes extremely rapidly (more than 40 breaths a minute)
- Has persistently blueish lips or fingernails (babies can briefly turn blue from the cold, or from crying)
- Has a cough that lasts longer than two weeks, or has a whooping or barking cough
- Has eye inflammation or discharge
- Has a rash that covers much of his body

## In the Medicine Cabinet

You'll be treating a lot of minor illnesses, so have the following to hand. For non-prescription medicines, check the label for the correct dosage. If no information is given for your baby's age or weight, ask the pharmacist or your health visitor or doctor.

- Thermometers
- Infant acetaminophen drops or suspension
- Infant ibuprofen drops
- Topical anesthetic (this is useless for teething, but may help with splinter removal)
- Vaseline
- Pedialyte

- Benadryl (an antihistamine, for allergic reactions)
- Dextromethorphan-containing cough syrup
- Calibrated syringes or droppers for giving medicine
- Nasal aspirator
- Saline nose drops
- Nappy rash cream
- Hydrocortisone cream
- Surgical spirit
- Oatmeal bath, soothing for many skin problems

## Fever Basics

'Does she have a fever?' That is one of the first questions you'll be asked whenever you call your doctor with a question about a sick baby – and it will soon be one of the first questions you'll ask yourself. Eventually, you'll learn to make a pretty accurate estimate of your child's temperature by touching your lips or cheek to her forehead. But you'll still need to know some numbers.

### Thermometers

Make sure you have a glass thermometer, a digital thermometer, a disposable strip thermometer or an ear thermometer. You can take a baby's temperature under his arm (axillary), or by reading the heat off of his eardrum (tympanic). You can't, however, take his temperature orally; holding the thermometer under his tongue would be uncomfortable and he might retch or choke. If you use a glass thermometer, your baby might bite off the end.

I'm a fan of digital thermometers. They have flexible rubber tips and beep when they are done. I find glass thermometers hard to read, and worry (probably needlessly) about breakage. Disposable strips are popular, as they are quick and easy to use, but they aren't very accurate and are not generally recommended by doctors. Ear sensors are expensive and are not considered reliable for use in babies under six months of age, because their ear canals are so small it's hard to get accurate readings from the eardrum. But they can be a plus for older babies because they work fast (insert the thermometer into your baby's ear while you open the ear canal by pulling on the earlobe, press the button, and wait for the quick beep). You can increase your accuracy by taking multiple readings and using the highest one.

## Taking Your Baby's Temperature

First, feel your baby's forehead and see whether his cheeks look flushed. he may also be sweaty, especially around the back of the neck.

DO consult your doctor if you are worried about your baby's temperature. The younger the baby, the sooner you should seek medical advice, as it is important to establish the cause of the fever, especially in a young baby.

To take your baby's temperature under his arm, open up or remove his clothing. Put him in a comfortable position, lying in your arm or against your chest. Put the glass or digital thermometer or fever strip in his dry armpit and tuck his elbow against his body. Cuddle him, making sure he doesn't move his arm. (You can pace the floor with him, just keep his arm firmly over the thermometer.) Wait four minutes, or until the digital thermometer beeps its all-done signal. Normal body temperature, taken from the mouth, is about 36.5–37°C (96.7–98.6°F). Axillary temperature is about 0.5°C (1°F) lower than this.

## How to Treat a Fever

If your baby has a fever, make sure he isn't dressed too warmly and that his room isn't hot. You can strip him down to his T-shirt, but keep a light blanket handy for when his temperature begins to drop.

With your doctor's permission and confirmation of the dosage, give him a fever-reducing medicine, like paracetamol or Ibuprofen.

You can also try to bring your baby's fever down by giving her a bath in a few inches of lukewarm water, using a flannel to spread water over her, then let her air-dry. You can also soak a towel in vinegar and place it on her feet, or sponge her head and limbs with lukewarm water.

Give your feverish baby lots to drink – she's sweating out fluids, and dehydration can make her temperature jump. One beverage you might try on a baby already drinking fluids other than breast milk or formula is catnip tea; catnip is a natural fever reducer.

Take your baby's temperature every couple of hours. If the fever doesn't reduce without medication, call the doctor.

## When Not to Treat a Fever

Remember that a fever is not an illness in itself. Fevers do have a purpose – they are part of a body's defenses against illness, although the exact mechanism is unclear. They may increase the number of white blood cells (which kill viruses and destroy bacteria) or raise the amount of interferon, an antiviral substance, in the blood and thus hinder bacteria and viruses from multiplying. Fevers aren't dangerous in themselves (although they serve as a warning of problems) except at extremely high levels – above 41.1°C (106°F). Mustering all your forces to bring your baby's temperature down every time she gets a fever isn't necessarily a good idea, and may, in fact, prolong her illnesses.

You'll develop your own system as you work out the way your child's body works – and every one is different. We are continually amazed when we have a kid with a high fever for 24 hours who then bounces up the next morning feeling great, having vanquished a cold virus that, in us, lingers for weeks.

You will notice that your baby's fever will climb in the afternoon from a morning low. This is normal, and doesn't mean your baby is getting worse.

## Febrile Convulsions

You should, however, be aggressive in fighting fevers in children who are susceptible to febrile convulsions. 1 to 2 per cent of children, most between five months and five years old, are susceptible to these kinds of seizures, characterized by symmetrical rhythmic convulsions, eyes rolling back in the head, and a loss of consciousness. The convulsions can last as long as ten minutes, but usually disappear in less than two minutes. Although it's less common, some susceptible children experience them every time they get a fever. The seizures usually have no permanent effects.

If your child has a seizure, turn him on his side, remove any hard objects he might bash into, and look at your watch. You need to time the seizure – your doctor will want to know its duration. If the seizure lasts longer than five minutes, call your doctor or hospital paramedics. After five minutes the child should get emergency care and be evaluated; but seizures of that duration are rare. If your child is prone to these seizures, you will probably want to administer fever-reducing medicine sooner, rather than later.

## Giving Medicines

'Give him one dropperful of paracetamol syrup' or 'Give her one teaspoon of antibiotic', your doctor says. You dutifully fill the dropper or syringe up to the correct line, put it in your baby's mouth, and squirt it in. It immediately comes dribbling back out, at which point you madly try to shovel it back in with your finger. Giving a baby medicine is not intuitive. If you're lucky, your baby will like the taste and lap it up – but don't count on it.

The UK government's medicines safety watchdog recommends that children under the age of 16 do not take aspirin in any form, unless specifically on the advice of a doctor. There is a link between aspirin ,and Reye's syndrome, a serious neurological disease. It is also thought that aspirin may pass into breast milk, so nursing mothers should also avoid the drug.

I was on my second baby before I knew how to give medicine so that it didn't dribble out, thanks to a paediatrician who insisted on drilling her favourite technique into me before she let me out of her office. Some may differ with this technique, and if you've got a method that works for you, by all means, stick to it. This two-person strategy worked for me.

One adult sits on the floor, leaning against a wall, with her legs straight out in front of her. Another adult lays the baby on the first adult's legs, so his head is slightly higher than his body (which happens naturally since your thighs are fatter than your ankles), and the baby's feet pointing towards the adult's feet. The first adult then lifts the baby's arms above the baby's head; this keeps his hands from knocking the medicine away and opens up his throat. The second adult slips the dropper or syringe into the side of the baby's mouth, between his cheek and where his molars will eventually appear, squirts in just a few drops of medicine, then a few more, and then a few more until the dropper is empty. It doesn't matter if the baby's mouth is shut or if he's crying; the medicine will dribble down his throat.

The first few times we tried the reclined technique, my kids screamed and squirmed – but it worked. After that, to my amazement, at medicine time they settled down immediately as soon as they were put into position.

Another method is the cheek pocket. Use a finger to pull out a corner of your baby's mouth to make a pocket in his cheek, and drop the medicine into the pocket a little at a time. Keep the pocket open until all the medicine has been swallowed.

WARNING: Get the dosage right. Double-check the dosage with your doctor, and make sure you are identifying the medicine correctly. Infant drops, for example, are much more potent than regular liquid medication. Medicines must always be measured carefully – never guess the amount.

Distraction can help make the medicine go down. If you can call on another adult or sibling to wave a toy or make faces at your baby, do so. Otherwise, dangle a toy from your mouth as you use both of your hands to give the medicine.

What you don't want to do is try to hide your baby's medicine in a bottle or in food. It still won't taste great, and if your baby doesn't finish the juice or food, you'll have no idea how much medicine he consumed.

If giving your baby medicine orally is always a struggle, ask your drugstore for acetaminophen suppositories. The dosage, in milligrams, is the same as that for oral medication, but is less preferable than the oral form, because the amount that is absorbed can vary.

## Eye Treatments

You may also, some day, find yourself having to give your baby eye medication, in the form of drops or ointment. You'll need to have someone hold your baby's hands so she doesn't rub away the drops immediately, or wrap her in a blanket. Balancing your hand on her cheek, but being careful not to touch the dropper to the eye, aim the drops for the inside corner of her eye. (Her eye does not need to be open; when she blinks, the drops will get in.)

If you're administering ointment, you do not need to force her eye open. Instead, squeeze out a line of ointment along the roots of her upper eyelashes (a bit like eyeliner). Keep her hands away from her eyes until the ointment melts into them. Alternatively, pull down her lower eyelid to make a pouch, and put the drops or ointment inside the pouch. If your baby really fights the eye medication, try applying it when she is asleep.

## Healthy Baby Care Tips

- Whenever you change your baby's clothes, touch your lips to her forehead. You'll get to know her normal temperature this way and will be able to quickly assess her for fever when she's ill.
- Bubble baths can be fun for older babies, but if your baby is a girl, you might want to make them a rare treat. Bubble baths can irritate the sensitive labial and vaginal tissues, causing itchy or painful rashes.

- Trust your instincts. If your baby's doctor dismisses your concerns but you feel something is wrong, don't back down. Insist that your baby be examined, until your baby is better or the cause of her symptoms is found.
- If your baby's illness includes vomiting or diarrhoea, line his crib with towels – these are easier to peel off and wash than the sheets.
- If giving medicine is a major struggle, ask your pharmacist if the drug comes in any other flavours. Parents report that some cherry-flavoured medicines taste really nasty, and the same medicine in orange or another flavour is sometimes accepted more willingly.
- Try refrigerating baby's liquid medicines – they may taste better cold – but check with the pharmacist or doctor that this is OK.
- If your feverish baby is too fussy to nurse or drink from a bottle, wet a clean flannel, freeze it, then give it to her to gnaw on.
- Go for a drive. An ill baby may sleep better in the car than the crib.
- This is a tip for you – don't make reservations that can't be cancelled. That will be the night that your baby falls ill.

Your baby will be unwell, and you will get through it. Most of us have access to excellent health care. Use it, rely on your good sense, and know that your baby will probably be better in the morning.

Remember: babies can't tell you what's wrong with them, and the symptoms may be misleading. For instance, your baby may have diarrhoea or vomiting when the problem is not actually his stomach. If you are concerned, speak to a doctor, especially if your baby is very young.

Do not worry about troubling your doctor or being thought a nuisance – it takes time to know when your baby is ill, and it is better to err on the side of caution. However, do resist the temptation to ask for a home visit during the daytime – it is usually quicker to go to your GP's surgery than wait for a doctor to come to you, and taking your baby outside for a while won't do any harm

## Cold Strategies

Babies catch colds – a lot of colds – particularly if they have older siblings bringing cold viruses home from school. Until your infant is about two months old, you should try to protect him from exposure to non-family members who have colds. Babies this young really need their noses to breathe; they don't easily switch to mouth breathing when their noses are stuffy, and therefore can be very uncomfortable.

Most colds are mild. A cold typically lasts a week to ten days. It may start out with a fever, followed by stuffiness, sneezing and, sometimes, a cough. Don't try to guard your baby against catching colds forever or try to protect him from his siblings' colds. The former will drive you crazy, and the latter is impossible. Unpleasant as they can be, your baby needs to have a few colds in his first year. Exposure means that he will be less susceptible to cold viruses later on, when missing a few weeks of school may set him back. It turns out that exposure to germs during their first year of life helps make a child's immune system function correctly. A recent study funded by the US National Heart, Lung, and Blood Institute concluded that frequent exposure to other children (and their germs), particularly in the first six months of life, reduces the chance of a child developing asthma later on.

Make sure your baby drinks plenty of liquids. If you are nursing, nurse frequently. If your baby is on solid foods, offer a variety of liquids. A baby with a stuffy nose may prefer to drink from a cup since it's easier than from a bottle. You do not have to cut back on milk. Milk rarely increases the production of mucus, and any liquids your baby will drink are beneficial.

## Other Common Illnesses

### Vomiting and Diarrhoea

In babies, vomiting and diarrhoea are usually caused by viruses. Wash your hands often; viral diarrhoea is very contagious. If vomiting and diarrhoea continue after several feedings, your baby risks dehydration, so give her plenty to drink.

Diarrhoea and vomiting can be very dangerous in babies, so if your baby has more than a couple of loose bowel movements or vomits (more than normal milk possetting), call a doctor.

In addition, contact a doctor if:

- There are signs of dehydration, such as no urine in over eight hours.
- Any blood appears in the vomit.
- There seems to be abdominal pain that lasts for more than four hours.
- The vomiting continues for more than 24 hours.
- Your baby just seems really ill.

## Ear Infections

My son Alexander was never an easy baby, but one night he just wouldn't stop screaming. My husband ended up spending most of the night driving around with him in the car, the only thing that seemed to help him relax. In desperation, the next day I took him to the doctor, who quickly diagnosed what was to be the first of many ear infections.

Unlike stomach viruses, which announce themselves clearly (and messily), ear infections are harder to identify, at least until your child is old enough to say 'Hurts' as he points to his ear. He may pull on his ear or bat at it – but some babies do that anyway. He will probably be fretful, particularly when you try to lay him down, and may have trouble sleeping – but some babies are like that anyway. And he may eventually get a fever.

Your baby may have an ear infection if he is pulling at his ear, fussing more than usual, or seems uncomfortable when reclining (particularly if he exhibits any of these symptoms after a few days of a runny nose). Your doctor will look in your baby's ear and, if the ear is infected, will see a red eardrum that is bulging with the pressure of trapped fluid. If your doctor decides to prescribe antibiotics, the good news is that you'll see a change in your baby's behaviour within 48 hours. If the doctor wants to wait a day or two because signs of infection are minimal, don't push for unnecessary antibiotics.

To make your baby more comfortable in the meantime, give him paracetamol or ibuprofen to dull the pain, and soothe his ear with hot compresses. Wet a flannel with warm tap water, wring it out and hold it over the ear (or use a heating pad), and keep him in a sitting position. Bring in his car seat, and let him sleep in that or in the buggy. Pile pillows or books under the head end of the mattress if he's in his crib. (Lying horizontally increases the pressure on the ear.) Ask your doctor to prescribe anesthetic eardrops to numb the pain.

Some babies get ear infections constantly – whenever, it seems, they get a cold. This can be more than a nuisance; an ear infection may muffle your baby's hearing just when he is learning to speak. Children do outgrow ear infections as their Eustachian tubes enlarge and become firmer, which improves drainage.

Not using a dummy, particularly when your baby is awake, seems to reduce ear infections, although researchers are not yet sure why.

## Croup

Croup is one of the scarier viruses. It seems to come on suddenly, usually in the middle of the night. You'll know croup when you hear it – your baby will sound like a seal barking. Croup usually lasts for five to six days, with the worst symptoms at night.

In severe cases you may hear a raspy, vibrating sound when your baby inhales between coughs, and breathing becomes difficult. Try to lower your baby's fever by removing excess clothing or giving paracetamol or Ibuprofen. Do not give cough medicine. Steam used to be recommended to treat croup; however, there is little evidence of its efficacy, and there is a risk of scalding. You can also take her outside – cool, damp air can help her breathing, and the change of scene may calm her down.

If these efforts have no effect after 20 minutes, or she is struggling to breathe even when she isn't coughing, or can't cry because she can't get enough breath, or is having difficulty swallowing, call a doctor at once.

'This is the scariest one!' Kim said. 'The cough is the worst sound you have ever heard, and your baby is visibly struggling to breathe. Once you know what it is, it is easy to treat, but you will never forget the initial shock of your child struggling for breath. Fortunately, it is a very LOUD illness; you'd be hard-pressed to miss it.'

## Asthma

Asthma is another scary one. It can be caused by allergies or by a virus that inflames the lining of the bronchioles. Again, the attacks usually come on at night. The child wakes up and has trouble exhaling. She panics. You may hear wheezing as your baby exhales, or notice the centre of her chest, between her breastbones, pull inwards when she takes a breath. Call your doctor if the breathing problems seem severe, if she's breathing rapidly (more than 40 breaths a minute), or if her lips or fingertips turn blue. While you're talking to the doctor, sit your baby up and try to calm her down; crying only makes her struggles to breathe worse. Always see your doctor if you suspect your child has asthma.

# Infectious Rashes

A number of infectious diseases are accompanied by a characteristic – and often uncomfortable – rash. As long as you breast-feed, and until about four months of age if you're bottle-feeding, your antibodies will provide some protection from any of these illnesses you have had.

As well as common infections, your child may come down with one of the rash-causing diseases you probably haven't heard of yet, such as Coxsackie virus, roseola and slapped-cheek disease.

## Coxsackie Virus

In Coxsackie virus, also called hand, foot and mouth disease, spots appear inside the mouth and on hands, feet and bottom. It usually comes with a fever, but the condition rarely causes long-term complications. Your baby will probably be miserable, as the mouth spots often blister, making swallowing uncomfortable. Keep nursing your younger baby; you can give an older baby juice ice lollies to help soothe her throat. She might be happier drinking from a cup than a bottle, and for older babies you can try putting half a teaspoonful of a liquid antacid in front of her mouth after meals. A Coxsackie virus bout can last as long as a week – and it makes for a very long week.

Coxsackie is very contagious from about two days before the rash appears until about two days after, with a three-to-six-day incubation period. Because it's hard to prevent spreading this one and it is generally harmless, doctors don't advise driving yourself crazy trying to quarantine your child.

## Roseola

The first symptom of roseola, or rubeola, that you'll notice will be a very high fever, as high as 40.5°C (105°F). The fever lasts for three to four days, and there are rarely any other symptoms, so you may have no idea what is wrong. Then the fever will go away and faint pink spots appear on your baby's trunk, neck and arms. This is good news – unlike the other rash diseases, the spots signify the end, not the beginning, of the virus. It is contagious until the rash is gone; the incubation period is about 12 days. There are no complications with roseola.

## Slapped-Cheek Disease

With slapped-cheek disease, your baby's face will be bright red, as if her cheeks were sunburned. The rash travels to the arms and legs, then on to other parts of the body. It usually lasts for a few days, but may go on for weeks, reappearing whenever she gets warmer than usual, when taking a bath, for example. Again, this is a fairly benign virus, and causes complications only in pregnant women.

You should keep your baby away from pregnant women. However, this can be tricky. Fifth disease is mainly contagious for a week before the rash appears. Once the rash appears, she is no longer considered contagious. If you believe a pregnant woman has been exposed to your baby, tell her to see her doctor. Slapped-cheek disease doesn't cause birth defects, but some infected foetuses develop severe anemia, and a small percentage die.

### Other Rashes

A rash may also be non-viral in origin. Cynthia rushed to the doctor when she saw spots all over her baby's face, suspecting chickenpox. Clare, it turned out, had been bitten by a mosquito.

Babies also typically get blotchy, red pimples in their second or third week. This baby acne is normal and goes away on its own. Heat can also cause a rash, particularly around your baby's neck, armpits or nappy area. Be sure not to overdress her when the weather is hot and humid. To soothe heat-induced rashes, give your baby a cool bath every few hours, letting her skin air-dry. Or, for small areas, lay a cool, damp flannel over the area for ten minutes or so at a time.

## Minor Ailments

The following are more of a nuisance than a crisis, but can cause problems if not treated:

- **Blocked tear duct.** A baby with a blocked tear duct (the little opening at the inside corner of the eye) looks like she is continually crying. Your baby's doctor will show you how to massage the area to open the duct. If this doesn't work after many weeks, the doctor may suggest having an ophthalmologist open the tear duct.
- **Eye infection.** If not kept open, as discussed, blocked tear ducts can turn into eye infections. Sometimes, of course, eye infections can appear out of nowhere. You'll see a watery discharge that clumps in your baby's eyelashes and sometimes seems to glue her eye shut. First clean the eye – dip a cotton ball in clean water and wipe the eye from the inside corner to the outside. Repeat until the eye is clean, using a fresh cotton ball for each swipe.

  You can also treat an eye infection with breast milk – squirt it directly from the breast into the eye several times a day for mild infections. For more serious infections, wash the eye thoroughly with a spoonful of expressed breast milk five or more times a day and call your doctor. If the redness lasts more than seven days, or if the outer eyelids are swollen, call your doctor.

- **Conjunctivitis.** Babies with conjunctivitis have yellow discharge along with red, irritated-looking eyes. Call your doctor for antibiotic drops or ointment. You can apply cold compresses to soothe the eyes and reduce swelling. Conjunctivitis is highly contagious, so wash your hands frequently and thoroughly to avoid giving it to yourself or your family.
- **Eczema.** These dry, red and extremely itchy patches most commonly appear in the creases of the elbows, wrists and knees, but can appear anywhere on the body. Eczema simply comes with sensitive skin, which is inherited, and flares up when the skin is irritated or from food allergies. If your baby gets eczema, use soap infrequently and detergent sparingly. Avoid woollen clothing, moisturize her frequently, and when she's going through a severe bout, dab a prescription cream on the scaly patches.

## Surviving Your Baby's Illnesses

Clear your calendar and put away the 'to do' list. If you work, call in sick. Given the amount of sleep you're probably getting, this is not a lie.

Your baby will want to be held most of the time. When he actually does fall asleep somewhere other than your arms, you'll need to lie down yourself and rest. You'll be getting a lot less sleep at night when your baby is ill, and will probably be fighting a bug yourself.

### Use Your Energy Wisely

Don't clean, don't cook, and don't do laundry (except for anything that's been pooed or thrown-up upon). Expect your baby to regress a stage. A baby who has been eating solids may only want to nurse; a baby who gave up his bottle for a cup a month ago may want his bottle again. Don't fight it – let him have what he wants now.

Your baby may wake several times a night, sometimes for hours. Don't pace the floor in the dark, bored and frustrated that you can't put her down and go back to sleep yourself. Discover late-night television. Find a trashy show that in your exhausted state of mind strikes you as funny (reality TV *can* be entertaining). Or make a nest of towels on the floor and lie down with your baby. This way, your bed won't get covered by snot or vomit, and maybe you'll both get some much-needed sleep.

Taking care of a baby is hard; taking care of an ill baby is harder. Admit it, and don't try to carry on with your normal activities.

Use the telephone. Call your mother, and cry to her. Call a faraway friend and complain to her about how hard it all is. Call your nearby friends and tell them how miserable you are (maybe some of them will offer to drop off a meal).

Remember: even though your baby is up all night crying, even though every sheet and blanket in the house needs a good wash, even though the only thing that calms him down is skipping up and down the hall – this will pass and you *will* sleep again.

## Vaccinations

In the UK, babies receive their first vaccinations at two, three and four months old. Your health visitor or baby clinic will inform you in writing when your baby is due for immunizations. Many parents of premature babies worry that their child will be too immature to cope with the vaccines, but UK advice is to follow the normal vaccinations timetable. Vaccines are not given before the baby is two months old, as antibodies from the mother may prevent the vaccine from working properly.

In the first year of your baby's life, she will be offered the following vaccinations:

**2 months:** Polio (by mouth); Diptheria, Tetanus, Pertussis and Hib (one injection); Meningitis C (one injection)

**3 months:** Polio (by mouth); Diptheria, Tetanus, Pertussis and Hib (one injection); Meningitis C (one injection)

**4 months:** Polio (by mouth); Diptheria, Tetanus, Pertussis and Hib (one injection); Meningitis C (one injection)

## Side Effects

Some children will have a reaction to some of these vaccines. A low-grade fever, soreness at the injection site and a mild rash with the rash-disease vaccines are typical. Serious reactions are few.

Immunizations should not be delayed for children experiencing ordinary cold symptoms, but if your child is feverish, you should delay the vaccination until she is better.

Getting the injection may actually be harder on you than your baby. She will probably let out a loud yell but be soothed fairly easily. Try to stay calm yourself – she'll pick up on your reaction. Consider stripping your baby to her nappy and pulling your shirt up. A recent study has shown that babies who had whole-body, skin-to-skin contact when their heels were pricked for a blood test had lower heart rates and didn't cry as much as other babies.

If your baby seems uncomfortable, is particularly fussy, or runs a fever in the day or two following the vaccine, medicate with acetaminophen. (If your baby typically has a reaction to a certain shot, you may want to premedicate.) If she develops a high fever or high-pitched screaming, she may be having a serious reaction; call your doctor.

CHAPTER 13

# Playtime

For the first few weeks of her life, your baby will mostly eat, sleep and use an incredible number of nappies. Then, after she's a few weeks old, you may find that she's not tired, hungry or wet, but she's still fussing. Why? Simply because she's bored.

## Why Play?

Once your baby tells you she's bored, it's time to introduce her to the concept of playtime. OK, she's only a month old, and she doesn't seem to be able to do much of anything. Work with what she's got – hearing, sight, a sense of touch, a sense of smell and some muscle control. Play that appeals to these abilities will entertain your baby and enable her to develop her mind and body.

Play is actually necessary for development. Play with others gives babies a chance to connect with them. Play with objects gives babies a chance to discover that they are powerful and that they can act on their environments. Solo play gives babies a chance to connect with themselves, and it will give you a few minutes while your baby happily entertains herself.

I wasn't that great at letting my first son, Alexander, entertain himself. He'd do about five minutes in his bouncy chair while I folded laundry next to him, but that was about as much of a break as I could get. I thought I couldn't expect much more. Then I visited a neighbour with a baby the same age – and she served me scones she had just finished baking. Her two-month-old baby hadn't taken an early nap. Rather, she had her house set up with play stations – an infant swing, positioned to look outside; a baby chairwith a view of the kitchen; a quilt on the floor with a few toys scattered on it. She moved her baby from station to station and this way could keep him happy and amused for as much as an hour.

## The Toy Box

You don't need a lot of commercial, primary-coloured plastic objects to entertain your baby. Besides, whether or not you fill a shopping trolley at the toy shop, you'll soon find out that you have more of those toys than you ever wanted (I think the things reproduce at night, like clothes hangers). Some of the best baby toys are things you already have around the house.

Once your baby can sit, she'll love playing with containers. Plastic food storage containers work just as well as primary-coloured ones sold in toy shops. She'll play with them empty, but will like them even better with something to shake – water, sand, oatmeal and birdseed all have great shaking potential.

She'll like to empty your kitchen cabinets. Don't childproof everything. Instead, make sure one or more drawers or cabinets are filled with things she can safely empty out. (My children's favourite was cardboard tea chests.)

**How can I tell if toys are safe?**
All toys should meet British Safety Institute (BS) standards or carry the CE mark. You should also check the recommended age for toys and that there are no small parts – age guidelines are given for a reason.

She'll want your television remote control. She sees other people in the family jockeying for its possession – she'll know it's important. She won't be placated with a toy one, with its chunky buttons and bright colours. Dig up an old remote (you know you have one somewhere), remove the batteries, and tape the battery cover on.

When you do buy toys, stick to the classics. Some baby toys you remember from your childhood are still around – there's a reason for that. These toys typically can be played with in a variety of ways and will interest your baby for years.

## The Basics

You'll need a rattle. Even a very young baby, who instinctively grasps anything put into her hand, can wave a rattle. After you've used it yourself to teach her to follow sounds, it will be a great entertainer during nappy changes.

You'll want nesting cups that fit inside each other. This will be your baby's first puzzle. These cups can also stack, pour, be sorted into colours and be counted. They let her experiment with the ideas of inside and outside and bigger and smaller.

You'll want stacking toys – plastic or wooden rings that stack up on a post. And you'll need lots of blocks – for touching, tasting and banging together. Eventually, they might even be used for stacking.

You'll probably also want a toy that does something when a button or lever is pushed (a train spins around, a funny man pops up). These break the classic rule about toy flexibility, but they teach cause and effect, and babies love them. (A light switch fits into this category, but just how long do you want to hold your baby up so she can turn the ceiling light on and off?)

Avoid empty film containers. While babies love them – they are the perfect size to clutch in a baby fist and can be filled with interesting things to dump or shake – film containers absorb chemicals from film that your child should not be ingesting. Also avoid coins. Your baby may love to play with your change, but coins are a big choking hazard.

You will also, particularly toward the end of the first year, need toys that let your baby imitate your activities – bowls, spoons (if you don't want to sacrifice your own), a little stove, a toy telephone, dolls, a mop, a toddler-sized buggy or shopping trolley.

What you don't need are 'educational' toys designed to turn your baby into a child genius. Your baby has a huge curriculum she's covering in her first year as it is. Your job is to simply expose her to life, not drill her in her numbers. Sometimes it is hard to resist, so go ahead and teach, but she'll be better off learning her academics at a more developmentally appropriate time. Brain growth, recent research shows, does not stop in early childhood, as used to be thought. It continues throughout life, so really, there is no rush.

## Toys You Already Have

Look around the house; you are well stocked with infant toys, you just may not realize it yet. Babies like things that go inside other things, things with lids to open and close, and things that can be stacked or moved around. They like things with interesting textures or ones that make interesting sounds. Some of the best are:

- **From the kitchen:** Wooden spoons, measuring cups and spoons, pots and pans, plastic containers with lids, balls of greaseproof paper or aluminium foil (bigger than your baby's fist)
- **From the bathroom:** Clean make-up brushes, cloth nappies, empty tissue boxes filled with light scarves, empty baby wipe containers, nylon net bath puffs
- **Other stuff:** Coasters, napkin rings, socks rolled into balls or used as puppets, clean feather dusters, shoes, old wallets and credit cards
- **Filled clear plastic bottles:** Clear or coloured water, liquid soap, dry pasta, feathers, rice or anything else that fits, makes noise and looks fun (glue or tape the top on to prevent choking hazards and messes)

## Toy Safety

To be safe, make sure that any playthings meet these criteria.

- ❏ The paint is non-toxic
- ❏ It has no small detachable parts
- ❏ None of the edges or corners are sharp
- ❏ No bells and whistles are at excessive decibels (some toy trucks emit siren noises that rival those from real fire engines)
- ❏ No 'bean-bag' stuffing (the pellets that stuff them are a choking hazard, so stick to playthings stuffed with fluff)
- ❏ The toy doesn't have long or loose cords, strings or ribbons (avoid anything, including necklaces, that your baby can get tangled around herself – especially her throat)
- ❏ No cords are more than 305mm (12in) long
- ❏ The toy, and any detachable parts, are too large to fit inside a toilet-paper tube

## Multi-Purpose Baby Games

Use playtime to encourage development by providing lots of opportunity for practice. Get him out of his infant seat and onto the floor, give him interesting objects to look at and reach for, take him out into the world and tell him about the world he's seeing. Use baby games that combine several of the senses and teach important lessons.

- **Peek-a-boo.** Everybody likes to play peek-a-boo with a baby – probably because it gets such a great reaction. Cover your face with a baby blanket or cloth and whisk the cloth away, saying 'Peek-a-boo!' You can also cover a toy with the blanket and then make it reappear with a flourish. Or cover your baby's head and let him pull off the blanket and say peek-a-boo to you. This teaches object permanence – that when things are gone, they aren't gone forever.

- **Hide and seek.** Lay your month-old baby down in the middle of the floor and move around the room, talking to him. As he hunts for the source of the sound of your voice, he starts to associate sights and sounds. Once your baby is crawling, partially hide behind a couch or doorway and call him to find you. When he gets good at this game, hide completely, but still call out. Eventually your baby will be able to hunt you down without the help of your voice. This also teaches object permanence – when mum is gone, she will come back.

- **Ah boo.** Put your baby, facing you, on your lap. Look him in the eyes, say 'AAAhhh' then lean forward, gently bump foreheads and say 'Boo!' This teaches him to anticipate you – he'll soon join in by leaning forwards to meet you.

- **Ankle or knee rides.** Sit down and put your baby on your knees, facing you, or straddling your ankles, lying forward against your legs. Support him firmly under the arms as you bounce him gently (he shouldn't pop off your leg) to the rhythm of a favourite rhyme. This teaches him balance, rhythm and anticipation as he hears the same rhyme over and over and learns to expect his favourite part ('had a great fall'). A variation (and a great exercise for parents) is inverted knee rides. Lie down on a rug, and bring your knees up above your chest, holding your calves parallel to the floor. Put your baby stomach down on your calves, head peeking over your knees. You can bounce him with your legs, or rock him from side to side (again, make sure you hold him firmly).

Keep in mind that unless her muscles, brain and nervous system have matured to the required level, no amount of practice will get her to a milestone before she's ready. Don't drive yourself – or your baby – crazy by trying to push her to achieve every milestone as soon as possible.

## Social Butterfly

Child development may be most visible when it comes to physical growth and mobility, but, along with strengthening muscles and improving coordination, your baby is developing in other ways. He's working out his feelings about his world and about other people. Your baby needs friends his own age to encourage that exploration. Although he may not be old enough to do more than lie on a blanket and kick his legs, getting him together regularly with other babies who are lying and kicking is important.

### Playmates

Researchers used to think young babies didn't really interact, and all two-year-olds did was parallel-play (sit near and imitate each other, but not really play together).

My kids' behaviour didn't fit in with this theory. They made close friendships before they could talk (they'd wriggle like mad when they saw a friend in the park), and their friends' names were among the first words they said. And it is pretty hard for me to define the wild game of hide and seek that Mischa and his friend Karly have been doing since they could crawl – thundering from room to room, accompanied by shrieks and giggles – as merely parallel play.

Research has caught up with what a lot of parents know from observations. Peer relationships start early and are different from parental or sibling relationships. At two months those two babies on a blanket will probably just look at each other; at three months they may try to touch each other; at seven or eight months one may crawl over to the other (or over the other) and try to hand her a toy. In fact, for a while you'll think your child is wonderful at sharing, as she's trying to give toys to everyone (the 'No, mine!' stage comes later).

## Playgroups

If you do need encouragement to start socializing, there are two things to keep in mind. You'll stay a lot saner if you spend some time with mums of children the same age, and long-term studies have shown that children who form good friendships early do better in school later on.

Start a playgroup. Find out if there is a mothers' club in your area – most mothers' clubs sponsor playgroups. Attend a parenting class sponsored by your local hospital – 'graduates' of some of these classes form playgroups. Take a lot of walks, get the phone numbers of other baby-carrying mothers that you meet, and organize your own.

If you want to form your own playgroup, ask your health visitor to recommend other mothers.

Try to start out with at least five or six other mothers—that way, if one or two miss a session, you'll still have a quorum. Schedule your meetings at least weekly (you'll probably find that early-morning hours are best for infants, but you can shift the time as the babies get older and nap schedules evolve). While many playgroups successfully meet at parks, I've found the kids – and mums – interact best at playgroups hosted at the members' houses. The group is less easily scattered (and your baby will get the idea of sharing his toys before he even knows that they are his toys).

## Social Milestones

When just born, your baby will be able to recognize her parents' voices and the voices of other people that surrounded her mother during pregnancy – siblings (if she has them), the cast of her mother's favourite television show.

She will also be sensitive to the feelings of others, particularly her mother. She'll notice if mum's feeling tense, and will quickly become tense herself. (My babies were sure to wake up and cry out for attention whenever I even thought about having sex with my husband.)

By four to eight weeks your baby will probably be actively smiling in response to things that make her happy – like hearing her mother's voice. Around the age of two months she will probably turn her head in the direction of a parent's voice and spend many happy moments gazing directly into your eyes.

When your baby is around four months old, you'll hear her first laugh and will put yourself through all sorts of crazy antics trying to get her to repeat it. Also around four months, you'll be able to tell when she's excited – she'll squeal, wriggle or breathe heavily.

At around six months another emotion will emerge – anger. You'll discover that your baby's angry cry is much different from his tired or hungry cry. This one won't be as much fun for you as joy and excitement, but it's an important one for your baby, because anger is motivating. A child who is cross that his favourite toy has rolled out of reach is motivated to wriggle over to it, developing his motor skills. Around the same time, your baby will also begin to recognize the difference between an angry voice and a friendly voice, and react accordingly.

## Stranger Anxiety

Sometime around the six-month mark, but perhaps as early as four months or as late as eight, your baby will, for the first time, get upset when you try to hand him over to a stranger. Stranger anxiety will make your life more difficult for a while, but it is an important developmental step. It means that your baby has figured out that his mummy, daddy and the other people he sees every day are different from everybody else in the world. He knows that food, comfort and fun come from these people. He doesn't want a substitute.

You can get through stranger anxiety best by giving in to it. Warn people whom your baby doesn't see often to approach him slowly; recommend that they sit across the room, ignore him for a while and wait until he approaches them (or, if he's not mobile, shows interest in them) before coming closer.

You also need to monitor your emotions to make sure you're not sending the wrong message. When a stranger approaches you in the supermarket to comment on your beautiful baby, do you clutch him to you, or smile and tell your baby, 'That nice lady thinks you're sweet'? When you hand your baby over to a sitter, make sure it's a sitter you feel comfortable with; if you're anxious, your baby will be, too. Always say goodbye if you're leaving your baby in someone else's care. If you sneak out you might get away easy that one time, but you'll pay for it for months. Eventually, after your baby comes to trust that you are not going to give him to a stranger and realizes instead that these people are just more fun faces to gaze at, stranger anxiety will pass.

## Don't Leave Me!

Separation anxiety is different from stranger anxiety and usually strikes at around eight months. It starts when your baby first falls deeply in love with her primary caregiver, the person most often feeding and cuddling her. This person will be showered with adoring looks and joyous greetings, and be tortured by the baby's misery whenever he or she is out of sight.

Like most other species, human babies develop this passionate attachment just before they are about to move independently. (Want a duckling to follow you everywhere? Adopt it just as it's about to waddle.) Your baby realizes that she can be independent from you and is therefore afraid that you'll move away from her. And, frustrating as it can be, separation anxiety is a plus – it makes it less likely that your newly mobile baby will be moving herself out of your sight.

The best way of dealing with separation anxiety is to simply go along with it. If your baby is clingy, let her cling, or pick her up and cuddle her; if she wants to explore, smile and nod at her explorations from across the room. If she doesn't want to leave you, pick her up and move her from room to room as you go.

Once she's moving on her own, move slowly so she can catch up with you. In a couple of weeks her speed will have picked up, she'll be more confident of her ability to follow you, and therefore less panicked when you move. Or keep up a constant conversation if you step out of the room; if she can hear your voice, she may not be so worried. You can play hide and seek (peek out from your hiding place and call her) to get her used to you appearing and disappearing.

A 'lovey' – a special blanket or toy – might help you and your baby through this phase. The lovey will remind your baby of you when you're not around. My kids, unfortunately, never did become attached to a lovey and had to struggle through most separations unaided. (Although one babysitter found that wrapping my baby Mischa in one of my unwashed nightgowns seemed to calm him down.)

In short, don't count on going to the toilet alone soon. Separation anxiety will come and go for years; get used to it. My oldest is nine and still seems to follow me every time I go into the toilet.

Stranger and separation anxiety are normal results of your baby's growing independence and self-awareness. Be patient and understanding as these phases come and go.

CHAPTER 14

# Watch Your Language

You've been communicating with your baby since you found out you were pregnant. Now that she's here in the world with you, don't stop talking! The sound of your voice will comfort her as a newborn baby, and guide her as she grows. Reading, signing and telling stories to your baby are critical for successful development of her language.

## Talking for Two

In your baby's first year, her senses and muscles are programmed for quick development. But they can't develop without stimulation. In a famous experiment, kittens were blindfolded at birth. Some time later the blindfolds were removed. The kittens, who had physically normal eyes, were never able to see, because their vision was not stimulated during a developmentally critical period.

Of your baby's senses, the sense of hearing is most developed at birth. She began listening before she was born. She's used to the sound of your voice – and she likes it a lot. So talk to her. You'll find that you'll naturally raise the pitch of your voice and talk in a sing-song pattern – these are the sounds she wants to hear, and you automatically know how to make them.

As many as 4 in 1,000 infants have some form of irreversible hearing impairment. Those who get help before six months of age are likely to develop language normally. Your baby will have a basic hearing test at her six-week checkup.

You won't, however, necessarily know what to say. In fact, you might feel pretty silly talking to someone who doesn't talk back. But you'll get used to it. You shouldn't talk baby talk. You're better off saying 'blanket' than 'bankie', for example, to allow your baby to hear all the sounds of the language she will soon be speaking. You do, however, need to forget about pronouns for a while. Instead of 'I, you, he', say 'Mummy, Susie, Daddy'. Right now Susie's finding out that everything has a name; later she'll find out that lots of people can be called 'she' or 'you'.

Pretend you're the narrator of a show starring your baby. Whatever you're doing, describe it. 'Mummy is taking off Susie's pajamas. One snap, two snaps, three snaps, four snaps. Ohh! There's Susie's tummy. Mummy gives Susie's tummy a kiss. Kiss! Now Susie needs a new nappy. OK, here's the nappy now.'

If your baby responds with any kind of noise, act as if she's talking back. Pause to let her finish her comment, and then respond. You can have great conversations, and, for now, your baby will agree with anything you say. Enjoy this!

## Goo-goo, Ga-ga

A newborn communicates through crying, which will quickly turn into a vocabulary. If you've been listening attentively, you will probably be able to distinguish cries of pain, hunger and exhaustion. At around a month, you may find your baby imitating you by opening and closing his mouth when you speak.

Around six weeks or so, you'll begin to hear classic baby coos. These are strings of vowel sounds, like aahh, eeeh, uhh.

'Leila and I had our first conversation, mimicking each other's sounds, when she was six or seven weeks old,' said Sheila. 'We were at the supermarket, in front of the chicken breasts. Instantly, I felt that I was a member of a team, rather than a lonely mum carting around a self-absorbed infant. Leila was very pleased to have broken through to me, and I was in awe.'

| LANGUAGE MILESTONES | |
|---|---|
| **AGE** | **MILESTONE** |
| newborn | cries |
| 1–2 months | cries differently to communicate pain, hunger and exhaustion |
| 6 weeks–2 months | coos or oohs (vowels) |
| 4–5 months | understands his name |
| 4–8 months | babbles (consonants) |
| 9 months | understands 'no' |
| 10–12 months | babbles without repeating syllables |
| 8–14 months | points |
| 10 months | responds to a spoken request |
| 10–18 months | says first words |

Somewhere between four and eight months old, your baby will add consonants, like 'gagaga' and 'dadada'. Since the most common first consonants are *g, k, l,* and *d,* he won't, however, be saying 'mama' yet, unfair as that may seem. By ten months or so he'll progress from repeating the same syllable to babbling strings of different syllables in a cadence that sounds a lot like talking.

Meanwhile, he's learned to understand his name, the word 'no' and a few other simple words. Between 10 and 12 months he will respond to a simple, spoken request, such as 'Wave bye-bye' or 'Give me the ball'. (Enjoy this phase; in about another year he'll quite gleefully do the opposite of what you ask.)

Between 8 and 14 months he'll begin to point. That's a recognizable attempt at sign language, and, if you're interested in signing with your baby, a signal that he's ready to learn more signs (see page 180).

Sometime between 9 and 18 months he'll say his first words.

**Should I worry if my baby is slow to talk?**
Babies can't do everything at once. Some babies focus on motor skills first, and may get around to working on language later than a more sedentary baby. As long as he's hearing language, your baby is learning to talk, whether he demonstrates it at 9 months or 18 months. Ask your health visitor if you are concerned.

## Rhymes and Rhythm

Sometimes you'll feel like you've completely run out of things to talk about. That's why we have nursery rhymes. Babies love the rhythm of rhymes. They also like hearing the same rhyme over and over again, and come to anticipate what you'll say next. So you don't need to know a lot of them; a few basic ones are sufficient. You can also get a Mother Goose book out of the library and learn a few of the more obscure rhymes, just for fun.

# Nursery Rhyme Refresher Course

## Basic Rhymes

Jack and Jill
Went up the hill
To fetch a pail of water.
Jack fell down
And broke his crown
And Jill came tumbling after.

Rub-a-dub-dub
Three men in a tub
And who do you think they be?
The butcher, the baker, the candlestick maker
They all jumped out of a rotten potato
Turn 'em out, knaves all three!

Little Miss Muffet
Sat on a tuffet
Eating her curds and whey.
Along came a spider
Who sat down beside her
And frightened Miss Muffet away.

Hey diddle diddle
The cat and the fiddle
The cow jumped over the moon.
The little dog laughed
To see such sport
And the dish ran away with the spoon.

## Bouncing and Movement Rhymes

As I was walking down the street,
down the street,
down the street

A bumblebee (refrigerator, flower, kettle – name anything)
I chanced to meet,
Chanced to meet,
Chanced to meet.
Hi ho hi ho hi ho
Riga-jig-jig and away we go, away we go, away we go
Riga-jig-jig and away we go
Hi ho hi ho hi ho
(Repeat using another object)

To market, to market, to buy a fat pig
Home again, home again, jiggety-jig.
To market, to market, to buy a fat hog
Home again, home again, jiggety-jog.

Humpty Dumpty sat on a wall
Humpty Dumpty had a great fall
All the king's horses and all the king's men
Couldn't put Humpty together again.

The Grand Old Duke of York
He had ten thousand men
He marched them up to the top of the hill
And marched them down again.
And when they were up, they were up,
And when they were down, they were down,
And when they were only halfway up,
They were neither up or down.

Row, row, row, your boat
Gently down the stream.
Merrily, merrily, merrily, merrily
Life is but a dream.

## Finger (or Toe) Play Rhymes

These are baby's fingers (touch fingers)
These are baby's toes (touch toes)
This is baby's bellybutton (touch bellybutton)
Round and round it goes (draw circles on belly)

This little piggy went to market
This little piggy stayed home
This little piggy had roast beef
This little piggy had none
And this little piggy went wee-wee-wee-wee
All the way home

Pat-a-cake, pat-a-cake
Baker's man
Bake me a cake
As fast as you can.
Roll it, and fold it,
And mark it with a B,
And put it in the oven
for Baby and me.

Open them, shut them, (open and close hands)
Open them, shut them,
Give a little clap.
Open them, shut them,
Open them, shut them,
Lay them in your lap.
Creep them, creep them, creep them, creep them
Right up to your chin.
Open up your little mouth
But do not let them in.

Here sits the Lord Mayor (touch forehead)
Here sits his two men (touch eyebrows)
Here sit the ladies (touch cheeks)
And here sits the hen (touch nose)
Here sit the little chickens (touch chin)
And here they run in (touch mouth).

Head and shoulders, knees and toes, knees and toes.
Head and shoulders, knees and toes, knees and toes.
Eyes and ears and mouth and nose.
Head and shoulders, knees and toes, knees and toes.

## Baby Sign Language Basics

Introduce basic sign language as early as you'd like; your baby may be making signs as early as nine months. When my second child was seven or eight months old, I taught her a few simple signs at dinner time, when she was sitting in her highchair and her hands were free. She learned them quickly and continued to use the sign for 'more' long after she was also saying the word. (Despite my intentions, I didn't make signs with my third child – it seemed I never had a free hand when I was with him.)

Research has demonstrated that early use of sign language may encourage the development of spoken language. But the big bonus of a baby who signs is the potential reduction in frustration – and accompanying tantrums – because he can tell you what is bothering him.

Exactly what sign you use for a particular word isn't important, as long as you are consistent. You can make up your own, get a book of simple signs intended to be used with babies, use tutorials from the Web, or use a mixture of all three. Here are a few basic ones.

FIGURE 14-1: **All gone/empty**
Sweep your right hand over your
down-turned left hand.

FIGURE 14-2: **Down**
Move a pointing finger down.

FIGURE 14-3: **Drink**
Pretend to grasp an invisible cup, and
raise the cup to your lips.

FIGURE 14-4: **Eat**
Touch four fingers to your mouth.

FIGURE 14-5: **More**
With your hands in loose 'O' shapes, bring your fingertips together in front of you twice.

FIGURE 14-6: **Scared**
Place your hands open, fingers spread wide, against the front of your chest.

FIGURE 14-7: **Sit**
Move two fingers of one hand down to rest over two fingers of the other hand, both hands palms down.

FIGURE 14-8: **Tired**
With hands palm in, move them down from your shoulders and slump, or use the sign for 'bed' (shown); put your palm against your cheek.

## Reading Lessons

You should also read aloud. Read from baby books, or from whatever magazine or newspaper you'd like. When reading to your baby, remember that you're reading, seeing and interpreting for two. This is your best chance to provide editorial commentary!

Discuss the story as you go, pointing out pictures that relate directly to the story, or to familiar things. 'See the cat? That's just like Suzie's cat!' Ask questions about how or why things are happening in the story, and speculate as to what the answers might be. Really, just verbalize your own observations and processing.

Read the same book over and over if that's what your child wants. Even if you're bored and ready to move on – he's not. On the most basic levels, repetition develops memory and comprehension.

Reading out loud is a one-man show. Change your voice for different characters, act out noises and sounds, and exaggerate the pitch of your voice. The more animated you are, the more your baby will focus.

Finally, improvise. Your baby's favourite part may be something that you add. This could be your big chance to explore your wild theatrical or literary side.

**tips**

DON'T:

- Prevent your child from turning back in the book, even if you read the same page all night.
- Rush. It may take a while for your baby to settle into a story.

## Beyond Lullabies

Babies love music, so no matter how poorly you do it, sing – you will have an appreciative audience. Turn on the stereo to music you like. Your baby will probably like it too, whether it's rock or reggae or classical. You don't need to buy special tapes of baby music (unless you have a particular fondness for the sounds of *Sesame Street* or the Teletubbies song). Down the years you'll be listening to your kid's favourite music often enough. Now's your chance to get her to listen to your favourites.

If you have a wind-up music box (on a mobile, in a stuffed animal or freestanding) you'll use it a lot. Now – to entertain your baby in the crib or on the changing table, and later – when your baby figures out how to wind it up himself. (At twenty months my youngest, worked out how to operate the pull-down musical clown hanging from the outside of his crib. For several months, every night at bedtime, when I'd sit in the rocking chair and try to coax him into my lap for his goodnight book, he'd wind up his music box and dance instead.)

You'll also be using musical instruments for a long time. Your baby's first instrument will be a rattle. Initially, you'll shake it for her. Try shaking it on one side of her head, and then the other. After a while she'll start looking around, trying to work out what is making the sound. At about four months she'll be ready to hold the rattle for herself. At six months or so, she'll start banging rattles together to hear the different sounds that makes. At this point she'll be ready for more complex musical instruments – like drums or tambourines.

In addition to music, introduce your baby to animal sounds. If you hear a bird or a dog outside, imitate it. If you look at a book about animals, make all the sounds.

## Life of the Mind

Even though babies aren't quite ready to fill out IQ tests, researchers still know quite a bit about what is going on in their minds. Babies start to recognize their mothers' faces between one and two months. At two months or so they become interested in things beside themselves and their mothers – this is the time to get out the toys. (This is a useful development, because it means your baby can be distracted when she is fretful or fussy.)

Between the ages of three and four months your baby can understand that three objects are more than two. At around four months she learns to anticipate regular events. For example, she may open her mouth when she sees you getting out your nursing pillow or taking a bottle out of the refrigerator.

| INTELLECTUAL MILESTONES | |
|---|---|
| **AGE** | **MILESTONE** |
| 1–2 months | recognizes his mother or primary caregiver |
| 2 months | interested in things besides himself and caregiver |
| 3 months | can discriminate between the possible (block sits on table) and the impossible (block floats in air) |
| 3–4 months | understands that three objects are more than two |
| 4 months | demonstrates preferences |
| 4 months | anticipates events |
| 5 months | follows another person's gaze |
| 6–9 months | recognizes that his face in a mirror is a reflection |
| 8 months | understands object permanence |
| 8–9 months | can set a goal and ignore distraction while pursuing it |

At around four months she will start preferring certain people or certain toys to others. At five months or so she'll learn to follow another person's gaze – if you look up at an aeroplane, your baby will probably look up, too. Somewhere between six and nine months she'll recognize that a face that she sees in a mirror is her reflection, not another baby, and may spend hours exploring that phenomenon.

At around eight months she'll understand object permanence – that when you leave the room or a toy is hidden out of sight, it continues to exist. (You can test this understanding by hiding a toy under a blanket. Until your baby understands object permanence, she won't bother to look for it, but may cry because it's gone.) By eight or nine months, your baby will be able to set a goal (get a toy), make a plan to carry it out (crawl around the table), and ignore distractions (you calling her in the other direction) while she carries out her plan.

# CHAPTER 15

# Movin' and Groovin'

**Y**our baby is only three days old, but clearly she's a genius. She already knows how to grab your finger and move her feet as if she's walking. Well, OK, those are just reflexes. But hey, wasn't that a smile? Although babies don't smile in response to your smile until two months or so, you may catch a few smiles from a newborn baby.

## What's 'Normal'?

If this is your first child, you'll be eager to fill in that list, recording when she first rolls over, sits up and crawls. If this is your second or third baby, you'll probably have mixed feelings when she hits a milestone. You'll be applauding her achievement, but will be aware of how much it will change your life. (A baby who turns over is no longer easy to change; a baby who crawls needs a childproofed house.) And you may be mourning the passing of an earlier stage. I'd love to see my littlest one crawl again, but once he started walking, there was no turning back.

First mum or experienced mum, you'll be noting your baby's developmental milestones, and, whether you plan to or not, comparing them to those of your baby's peers. Odds are she'll do some things earlier than others, some things later, and once in a while will hit the median. You may be running to the DIY superstore for safety gates months earlier than you had expected, or wondering why your baby hasn't taken a step while other babies her age are jogging. She may be focused on learning to talk and will get to walking later. However she's progressing, don't forget that there is a wide range of 'normal'.

## Now You See It

At birth, sight is the least developed of the senses. Babies are nearsighted, and the world is pretty much out of focus. They focus best about 200mm (8in) from their noses, and can't see much beyond 460mm (18in) from their nose. Babies' vision develops at different rates; your baby may have nearly normal vision by six months, or it may take years.

In the beginning, babies prefer to look at faces – particularly their mother's face – more than anything else. So give your baby plenty of face time. Hold him on your lap and gaze at him; sit him in his chair and make faces at him.

Give him other things to look at as well, factoring in that critical 200mm (8in) distance for the first two months or so. You've probably hung a mobile over the changing table, and maybe another one hangs over the crib. But babies would rather look at something new than something they've seen before, so change these mobiles regularly (simple cutout shapes or pictures from magazines work well).

**Go sightseeing.** Carry your baby around the house, looking for things that, to a baby, would be a point of interest – a brightly coloured bouquet of flowers, a shiny kettle, a patch of sunlight on the carpet.

Take your baby on a flying tour. I have to credit Steve Wozniak, co-founder of Apple Computer Inc., for coming up with this idea and demonstrating it to me several years ago. You can do this as soon as your baby is strong enough to hold his head up on his own, while he's still light enough for you to carry easily on outstretched arms. Put one hand under his chest, fingers splayed wide so you can feel his muscles. Use the other hand to support his pelvis. Start near an interesting spot and hold your baby in the air. Then try to sense which way his muscles are trying to tug him. It may take you a few minutes, but you'll begin to be able to tell which way he wants to go. (Resist the urge to take him to where you see him looking, let his muscles guide you instead.) For people who didn't believe babies have minds of their own, Woz told me that he used to do a trick – he'd get someone to blindfold him, and throw a handkerchief on the floor. He'd then let the baby direct him to the handkerchief.

Stock up on baby bath. Bubbles move slowly, float in interesting patterns and catch the light; they'll give your baby lots of eye-tracking practice. Later on, he'll begin to try to catch the bubbles, developing his hand-to-eye coordination.

Use the mirrors in your house, or buy an unbreakable mirror for your baby to play with. Look in a mirror with your baby, make faces and label your expression (happy, sad, angry). Encourage him to touch the baby in the mirror – one day he'll work out that it's him and will be amazed. Act as a mirror for your baby. When he makes a face, you make the same face. He'll be thrilled with his power!

## Reach Out and Touch

When your baby is newborn, you'll be doing most of the touching. Remember that it's not just hands that can feel things. Sensitivity to touch develops from the top down – your baby's face will be able to distinguish different sensations sooner than her hands will. Use a make-up brush or large paintbrush to pretend-paint your child, talking about the parts of her body as you do it. Or stroke her with a cotton ball or even a terry nappy or blanket. You can keep a clean feather duster near your changing table, and 'dust' your baby when you change her. Blow gently on your baby's stomach, or kiss her toes.

### Self-Discovery

By two or three months, your baby will have found out that her hands belong to her and will watch them as she's playing with them, trying to reach out and touch objects. For a while her hands will be her favourite toy. You can vary this game by putting a brightly coloured sock or wrist rattle on one of her hands.

Once she's worked out that she has hands, it's time for batting practice. You can buy an official cradle gym (straps over the crib), baby gym (self-supporting and can be placed over your baby when she's lying on the floor), or a bouncy chair with a toy bar. All three of my babies would spend 15 to 25 minutes at a stretch batting at, and occasionally grabbing, the butterfly, little man and bunch of triangles attached to the bouncy chair. This was good practice in entertaining themselves, and provided plenty of time for me to eat breakfast.

By four months or so your baby will be tired of hitting things and will want to take them in her hands – and bring them to her mouth. Put a toy in your hand and hold it out to your baby – then be patient. It will take her a while to calculate the path from her hand to the object; if you rush to put the toy in her hand, you'll interrupt this process.

## Massage

Massage is a great way to relax some babies. (A few just don't like it; if yours falls in that category, don't force it.) And it is easy to do – you don't need special classes (although such classes abound).

For your baby's first few massages, just do her arms, hands, legs and feet (the face and chest are a lot more sensitive). Use a cold-pressed vegetable oil and warm it first by rubbing it between your palms. Avoid baby oil; it's made of petroleum, and you don't want your baby sucking it off her arm.

You might start with your baby's hand, perhaps with a finger play poem. Then rub her palm gently, starting with your thumbs in the centre and moving them out along the fingers. Do both hands, and, if she approves, move on to her feet. Remember to stroke very slowly, moving down away from her head.

*f@ct*

> Unlike adult massage, which pushes down into the muscles, baby massage is a surface massage, using gentle and smooth strokes.

For her chest, start with your hands in the center, and move them away from each other down to her sides, following the line of her ribcage. On her stomach, move your hands clockwise around her bellybutton (this is the direction in which the large intestine turns). (**Caution:** don't massage her stomach until her umbilical cord falls off and there is no redness in the area.) You can even do a gentle face massage, making small circles with your fingers around your baby's cheeks, stroking behind the ears, and smoothing her forehead outwards from the centre.

You don't need to know any fancy massage moves – slow, gentle stroking is really all it takes. If you want a few advanced moves, try:

- **Milking** – Gently tighten your hand around her leg as you pull down towards her foot.
- **Criss-cross** – Put one hand on each of her shoulders, stroke one hand down towards her opposite hip, and repeat with the other hand. Then reverse, going back up to the shoulders.

- **Rock-a-bye** - Put your hands gently on her stomach and rock her from side to side.
- **Bread dough** - Hold her arm between your two palms and roll it back and forth.
- **This little piggy** – —Rotate each toe of your baby's foot, then gently massage the sole of the foot with your thumbs.

## Dexterity Begins

At eight or nine months your baby will begin to use his fingers and thumbs separately. This is when the pincer grasp (thumb and forefinger) develops, and he can be happily entertained for long stretches (long in baby time, anyway), trying to pick up bits of food and put them into his mouth. At this stage he'll begin to feel things by rubbing them between his thumb and forefinger. Make a toy for the car by securely sewing together scraps of different types of fabric –silk, velvet, corduroy, lace.

He also will want to poke his index finger into things. A set of wooden rings, meant to be stacked on a rod, fascinated my babies at this age – they would hook their fingers through one in each hand and carry them as they crawled.

Soon after this stage your baby will start to learn how to let go of things (I called it 'testing gravity'"). You'll first notice it in the high chair, as your baby deliberately drops things off the side and expects you to pick them up – again and again and again. He acts like it's a game, and it is. If you don't want him playing it with his food, give him other opportunities to practice with beanbags, balls or blocks. (Place a basket under his highchair and encourage him to drop the toys in it – it will make cleaning up so much easier.)

By nine months or so, your baby may be ready to start scribbling. Readiness for this game doesn't hinge so much on whether your baby can hold a fat crayon or chalk and use it to make marks on paper,but on whether or not he still insists on eating the crayon or chalk. I've usually started my babies with white chalk on black paper; it takes a lot less pressure to get a piece of chalk to make a mark than it does a crayon, and white chalk is about as mess-free as it gets. (If you want to save these first scribbles, spray the paper with hairspray; just don't do the spraying anywhere near your baby.)

## Pump It Up

Get double duty from playtime. Your baby should have plenty of opportunities to kick on his back (you can hold a beach ball over him and encourage him to kick it). In fact the more time he has on the floor – in all positions – the better. Unlike car seats, swings and infant carriers, when he's on the floor, he's in charge of how he moves.

Tummy time is important from the beginning. A newborn baby placed on his stomach will try to lift and turn his head. He'll do little pushups and, as the months go on and his muscles develop, rock up onto his knees. Eventually, tummy time typically turns into crawling.

So, when your baby is awake and ready to play, you don't always need to recline him in an infant chair or lay him down on his back. The American Academy of Pediatrics recommends that babies spend some time every day on their tummies, with an adult nearby.

*fact*

Babies used to spend a lot of time on their stomachs because that's the way they slept. Now babies are put to sleep on their backs, and typically don't get much tummy time.

If you have a quilt (not a duvet, but a cotton eiderdown that easily lies flat), use it for tummy time. A bare floor is too hard; a carpet sheds fibres that end up being inhaled and swallowed. Lie down face to face with your baby, or put some toys in front of him to encourage him to pick his head up and look around.

Once your baby is crawling, use some couch cushions to create an obstacle course that he'll crawl around or over. Scatter a few toys around the room a short way away from your baby. Give him things that scoot out of his reach and beg to be chased – balls or light toys on wheels. Get down on your hands and knees and let him chase you, and then chase him back again.

Parent participation games also help your baby's muscles develop. Once his head control is solid, try swinging him. Pick him up by a wrist and ankle and gently swing him from side to side. Don't jerk him, however; you can easily dislocate his elbow. Do lift him up above your head while holding him firmly under his armpits. He'll look down at you and probably stretch out his arms and legs.

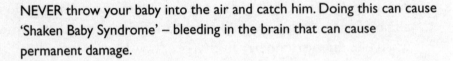

NEVER throw your baby into the air and catch him. Doing this can cause 'Shaken Baby Syndrome' – bleeding in the brain that can cause permanent damage.

Bicycle your baby's legs from the time he is an infant. Initially, you'll do all the work, but after a few months, he'll push against your hands as you move his feet. Eventually, you can cycle side by side.

Let him jump. Hold him under his arms and with the soles of his feet on your lap, lower him to bend his knees, and then lift him up into the air. Pretty soon he'll bend and straighten his legs himself – and he'll be jumping, though you'll support much of his weight.

## By the Numbers

No milestone chart can tell you what your baby will – or should – be doing at a particular age. Indeed, child development experts differ in their opinions of when milestones can occur. And those opinions change. Most babies roll over between four to six months of age. Less than ten years ago, more rolled over in the earlier part of that range than today; today's babies are sleeping on their backs and getting less practice pushing up on their arms and lifting their torsos than the stomach-sleepers of the past.

Hitting a milestone late or early doesn't mean much in the scheme of things. It doesn't correlate with intelligence. It rarely indicates a problem, although falling behind normal ranges in many milestones may indicate that something is up, and you should consult a paediatrician.

Tell your doctor if:

- Your baby consistently falls outside 'normal' milestone ranges
- Doesn't seem to use one side of his body
- Doesn't react to loud noises
- Doesn't react to bright light
- Doesn't realize the difference between familiar people and strangers by the age of ten months

Slower development may simply be a sign of your child's personality. Some children have more cautious personalities than others; some learn by watching rather than doing. A doer may walk sooner but take a lot of spills; a watcher may walk later with hardly a wobble. Your baby may hit a milestone sooner if she's around slightly older babies – there's nothing like peer pressure to get a kid motivated. (My daughter spent a morning at playgroup lying on the floor, watching the other babies crawl around her. She spent the afternoon at home rocking on her knees, and by that evening was crawling herself.)

Don't become obsessed about whether or not your baby is on some expert's schedule. The only schedule she's likely to be following is her own. But do be sure to applaud her every step of the way – babies thrive on enthusiastic audiences.

## The Motor Skills Milestones

The first voluntary muscle movement a baby usually makes is turning his head. The head turn, which you'll usually see in your baby's first few weeks, develops the neck muscles and starts the progression of muscle movements that several months down the line will allow your baby to turn himself over. (In my big-headed son's case, a head turn moved him over without any other muscle involvement when he was two weeks old.)

To encourage your baby's attempt at a side-to-side head turn, lie down next to him until he looks at you. Then jump up and run around him, and lie down on his other side until he looks your way again. This move is great for getting parents in shape, but if it's too much for you these days, put a toy or a mirror on one side of her and switch its position.

After the head turn comes the mini push-up, a move that takes a little bit of shoulder muscle to pull off. In the mini push-up, which your baby will probably conquer between the ages of two and four months, he will use his arms to lift his shoulders and chest (but not that big baby stomach) off the ground. He may be late reaching this milestone if he spends a lot of time on his back or sitting in an infant seat. For push-up practice, put him on his front on the floor, then hold a toy in front of, and slightly above, his head so he needs to lift himself up for a good look.

| MOTOR MILESTONES | |
| --- | --- |
| **AGE** | **MILESTONE** |
| Birth–1 month | side to side head turn |
| 2–4 months | mini push-up |
| 2–5 months | swipes at object |
| 2–5 months | brings both hands together |
| 3–7 months | rolls over |
| 3–7 months | grasps objects |
| 5–9 months | sits unsupported |
| 6–12 months | crawls (or somehow travels on four limbs) |
| 7–13 months | pulls up to a stand |
| 8–17 months | walks |

## The Swipe and Grab

Two early motor milestones that seem simple actually require developmental prowess to achieve: the swipe and the grab. You'll usually see this between the ages of two and five months. To perform the swipe and grab your baby needs to overcome one reflex he was born with: the tonic neck reflex. This reflex puts his arms in a fencing position – one arm extended, the other arm bent – whenever he is placed on his back with his head to one side. He can't get control of his hands until he can suppress this reflex and position both hands in front of him. Then he needs to recognize his hands as something he can control and bring towards other objects he can see.

To encourage him to swipe, use a baby gym. These are available for cribs, for floor play, and for infant seats. To encourage him to bring both hands together in a baby version of a clap, sit him in his baby chair and play pat-a-cake, clapping the rhyme with your own hands, and then with his.

From batting at objects, the next obvious step is grabbing them, and babies usually reach this milestone between three and five months. To voluntarily grab something, your baby needs to override the grasp reflex that makes him close his hands tightly whenever something touches his palms.

## Roll Over

The roll is not only a very noticeable milestone, but for many babies is their first attempt at independent motion. You'll see it sometime between three to seven months. A baby who spends a lot of time on his stomach may roll sooner rather than later, using the front-to-back roll. This is a fairly simple movement compared to the back-to-front roll. Babies who spend most of their days on their backs will probably roll later, starting with the back-to-front roll. Once your baby masters both rolls, you may be surprised one afternoon when you put him down in the middle of the rug for a little playtime, leave the room for half a minute, and come back to find him hiding under the coffee table.

To encourage your baby to roll, make sure he gets plenty of tummy time. If he's willing, roll him across the room like a rolling pin. You can also use a pillow or rolled blanket to prop your baby on his side, lie down on his other side, and tempt him to reach for you or a toy that you're holding. If he stretches his arm out enough, he probably will topple over. The roll will impress friends and grandparents, but will make your life more difficult, since you'll no longer be able to count on your baby staying where you put him.

## Sit!

The sit, which appears at an average of five to nine months and may arrive before or after the roll, will make your life a lot easier. A sitting baby has free hands and can entertain himself by picking up and dropping toys while you entertain yourself by, oh, doing the laundry or putting away dishes. (When you've had to do both jobs with a baby on your hip for six months or so, it *is* a thrill to do them with both arms free.)

For sitting practice, surround him with pillows for him to keep his balance, but stay close; he'll tip over and need to be rescued regularly. Or sit behind him, with him leaning back against you, and use his hands to pull him gently up into a sitting position.

## On the Move

The next big milestone for your baby, and a major life change for you, is the crawl. While a rolling baby can travel only a few yards at a time, a crawling baby can go just about anywhere – and you can be sure he doesn't like to be stopped.

This is the time to start serious childproofing. Start by getting down on your hands and knees and crawling around the room, thinking about what might hurt your baby. You'll see electric sockets, tangles of cables and wires, sharp corners of tables, the door to the oven, knick-knacks on the bookshelf, and oven cleaner under the sink. You may see upholstery nails sticking out of the underside of a chair, or tacks coming loose from under a sofa.

Your baby may scoot about in a sitting position, creep or 'commando crawl' (move around on her stomach, using her hands, elbows, knees and feet for propulsion, looking like a soldier scurrying under barbed wire), or 'elephant walk' (move around on all fours, but support herself on her feet instead of her knees). Not all babies do an official hand-and-knee crawl, and the widespread fear that a failure to crawl means reading difficulties later on has been put to rest.

Your baby may miss the crawling stage altogether and focus on learning to walk upright. In fact, this is becoming more common, with an increasing number of babies going directly from sitting to walking because they spend so little time on their stomachs. There seem to be no medical consequences to this change.

If you want to encourage your baby to crawl, put her in soft long trousers with cuffs to make crawling comfortable (she'll just get tangled up in dresses or loose trousers that are too long) and give her a beach ball or wheeled toy that easily rolls out of reach.

## Upstanding Citizen

Once your baby starts pulling himself upright, he'll be pulling up on every object in sight, even at night. Sometimes even babies who are great sleepers have a spate of interrupted nights when, barely half-awake, they pull up in their cribs and discover they don't know how to get down. Once your baby starts pulling up, begin teaching him how to bend his knees and sit down again. Standing supported, a skill your baby will probably demonstrate between the ages of seven and 13 months, takes the development of the muscles around his joints, general muscle strength in his legs and arms, some coordination and a sense of balance.

To help your baby in his standing attempts, keep him barefoot as much as possible: he'll be more confident about standing if he can feel the floor. Forget about shoes. Your baby doesn't need them to support his feet, and they get in the way rather than help when he's starting to stand and walk. If it's cold, put him in well-fitting socks with non-skid bottoms.

Thick carpet may give him trouble (even though it reassures you about falls), so let him practise on wood or linoleum floors. Make sure he has plenty of solid, safe objects to pull up on. (You might temporarily replace your glass-topped coffee table with an ottoman or wooden toybox.) Play games with him – —start with him on his back, hold his hands and slowly pull him to a stand.

## Walk This Way

After standing comes walking, at eight to 17 months. Heavy babies may be on the late end of that spectrum, adventurous babies may walk on the early side. The level of parental protectiveness does play a role; try to reign in your fears. Early walkers may fall more often than their later-walking peers, but are unlikely to get seriously injured.

Julie's baby, Willy, didn't start walking until the end of his 16th month. Julie had been worried for some time and told herself that when he reached 17 months she was going to consult a specialist. But one morning Willy walked across the living room with no trace of a wobble, and was soon running. Julie thinks much of the delay was due to his cautious personality.

**What if my baby's walking oddly?**
The duck-walk (legs spread wide apart and toes turned out like a duck) helps a shaky walker keep his balance. Most babies are naturally pigeon-toed, and some have shins or thighs that just tilt a bit. My kids' perfectly normal bowlegged walks panicked my mother, who grew up when bow legs were a sign of a nutritional deficiency. Other babies seem to always walk on their tiptoes. If you are concerned, ask your health visitor or GP, but the odds are that it's simply a matter of style.

To encourage your baby to walk, simply move just out of reach, hold out your arms, and call him toward you. Some babies learn to walk by wheeling push-toys around. If you think all your baby needs is a little confidence, hand him a toy when he is standing, and he may think that he is holding on to something supportive and take a step. My son Mischa took his first steps clutching a garden hose in both hands, clearly convinced that it was holding him up.

## Try This

- **One month:** Place your face about 305mm (12in) from your baby's face and move slowly from left to right, letting your baby's eyes track your movement.
- **Two months:** Purchase a wrist rattle, or securely sew a bell onto a baby sock. Put the rattle or sock on your baby's hand and watch as she

discovers the connection between her hand movements and the sound the bell or rattle makes.

- **Two months:** Say hello to your baby every time you enter a room in which she is. She'll recognize your voice and soon come to anticipate your arrival.
- **Four months:** Put a toy just out of your baby's reach – you may find that she can somehow wriggle or roll her way to it. (But don't frustrate her ; if she doesn't get it in 15 seconds or so, hand it to her.)
- **Five months:** Whenever you're about to pick up your baby, hold out your hands and say 'up'. Pretty soon she'll be reaching toward you as soon as you say the word.
- **Five months:** Draw a simple picture of a smiling face on one side of a paper plate, and a mixed up, Picassoesque face on the other. Hand your child the plate; she'll quickly work out which side she prefers to look at.
- **Six months:** Drape a blanket or terry nappy over a favourite toy, leaving a bit of the toy peeking out. Your baby will be thrilled when she 'finds' her toy.
- **Six months:** If your baby is crawling confidently, make her an obstacle course of pillows and couch cushions to crawl over and around.
- **Eight months:** Let your baby watch you as you hide a toy under a blanket for her to find.
- **Eight months:** Show your baby how to put a lid on a pot. After she masters this puzzle, give her two lids and two pots.
- **Nine months:** Put a piece of sticky tape lightly on your baby's hand. Let her work out how to peel it off.
- **Nine months:** Put several simple but distinct toys in front of your baby. Ask her to hand you one by name: 'Give Mummy the ball', holding your hand out. You may be surprised that she gets it right.
- **Ten months:** Hand your baby a toy for each hand. Then hold out a third toy to her and see what she does. Will she try to somehow hold all three toys, or drop one of the two in order to pick up the third?
- **Twelve months:** If your baby is walking, give her a barefoot tour of different surfaces such as carpet, floor, grass and sand.

- Enjoy today's stage of development (and take pictures); it may not last until tomorrow.
- Don't compare your child to anybody else's. Such competitions can be, at best, annoying and, at worst, damaging to friendships and, potentially, your child's self-esteem.
- To turn ordinary socks into non-skid socks for beginning walkers, scribble on the bottom with '3D' fabric paint, available inexpensively at most habadashers or fabric shops.

CHAPTER 16

# Childproofing and Safety

n addition to coughs, sniffles and sneezes, you'll have to deal with the bumps and bruises your baby will encounter, despite your best efforts. He'll increase his exposure once he's mobile, but even infants can get bumped, burned or scratched.

## First Things First

Before you buy a lot of childproofing gear, do the simple things. If you don't want your books all over the floor, replace the books on the lower shelves with your baby's books, or stuff extra books in each row until they're jammed in too tight for him to move. Gather up any poisonous items, from detergent to vitamins, and put them on your highest shelves (locking a cabinet works only if you always close the lock). Cut looped blind cords into separate strands to reduce the choking hazard, or knot them up out of reach.

- Try making one room completely childproof, and put a gate on it. Then you can use it as a giant playpen when you need to contain your child.
- Don't childproof absolutely everything in every room. Remove the hazards, but leave a few things out that would be inconvenient (a torn magazine cover, for example) but not disastrous if your baby got into them. Use them as tools to teach your baby that some things are OK for her to play with and some things are not. You don't want to frustrate your baby by telling her 'No' all day, but she needs to understand the concept, or you won't be able to take her out much.

If you have glass-topped coffee tables, put them away, or put away any heavy objects that could be used to smash the glass (although you may be surprised – my first son smashed our glass-topped table when he dropped a bongo drum onto it). Put away your tablecloth and invest in a set of place mats. If you sew, put your sewing basket up on a high shelf, and make sure you unplug your sewing machine and put it away every time you use it.

Make sure you can identify all your houseplants (if you have to, take a leaf to a local garden centre) and confirm that they are non-toxic. Turn your water heater down to the lowest setting, if you haven't already. Put at least one waste-paper bin in a locked cabinet, and think before you throw things into accessible waste-paper bins (avoid things like empty containers of cleaning products or used disposable razors or blades).

House guests may not be as aware of childproofing as you are. Remind them to keep jewellery, make-up bags, shaving kits and medicines out of your baby's reach. Elderly guests, in particular, often don't keep their medication in childproof containers.

Make a list of the childproofing gear you need to get. Don't buy everything in sight; you may be wasting your money, since some babies have no interest in toilets, doorstops or stereo wires.

Start with stairs, which will probably need stairgates, as will any rooms that you plan to keep off-limits. Gates that screw into the walls are better than pressure gates, particularly at the top of the stairs. (You don't want a pressure gate giving way when your baby flings himself against it – and he will.)

You'll probably also want to get socket covers, either for unused sockets or ones that block access to the plug for sockets you use frequently. You don't need cable shorteners – use twist ties, and forget about cable guards - use wide masking tape. (Buy the more expensive type, which is less likely to damage your paint.) If your child is tall enough to reach doorknobs, consider installing a chain or latch, high out of reach, on doors that lead outside.

## Basic Childproofing

### For Crawlers:

- Cover electrical sockets
- Remove or block access to furniture that is easily tipped over (such as floor lamps)
- Move breakables or dangerous knick-knacks out of reach
- Regularly hunt for dropped coins or other potential choking hazards
- Hide, coil, cover or block access to electric cables
- Knot blind cords out of reach, or cut through loop
- Install stairgates

- Make sure pools and fish ponds are covered; toilets should be locked. Don't even leave a pail of water unattended.
- Give the lower shelves of your bookcases over to your child; move your books out of reach, and stock the shelves with baby books.

### Additional Childproofing for Cruisers and Walkers

- Install window guards if you live in a flat or a house with upper floors
- Lock kitchen cabinets and drawers that contain anything dangerous (knives, etc.)
- Turn pan handles toward the back of the stove when cooking
- Make sure bookcases will not topple over
- Secure the TV so it won't fall if tugged on or pushed

## Your Shopping List

Whether or not you need these items depends on the layout of your home and your childproofing decisions. For example, do you want to put latches on your kitchen cabinets, or rearrange the contents so that all hazardous and breakable items are stowed high out of reach, and store only child-safe items (pots and pans, Tupperware) in the lower cabinets?

- ❏ Socket covers or caps
- ❏ Stairgates
- ❏ Drawer and cabinet latches
- ❏ Toilet lock
- ❏ Foam strips or corners for table edges
- ❏ Window guards
- ❏ Window latches
- ❏ Oven lock
- ❏ Doorknob covers
- ❏ Stove knob covers

## So You Think It's Safe. . .

When you think you've thought of everything, watch your child to see what hazards she discovers. Is she fascinated by the oven door? You may have to strap it closed. Does she like to throw toys in the toilet? You may want a toilet lock, but since these are difficult for older siblings or uninitiated guests to operate, you may prefer just to keep the bathroom door shut. Is she climbing the bookshelves? Make sure they are bolted to the wall. Some babies simply require more childproofing than others. You'll soon discover what kind of adventurer lives in your home.

### Top Ten Household Dangers

10. Poisonous plants
9. Venetian blind cords
8. Electric cables and wires
7. Electric sockets
6. Stoves, heaters and other hot appliances
5. Poisonous household products
4. Medicines
3. Water (even water in a bucket used to mop the floor is a hazard)
2. Coins or other small objects (choking hazard)
1. Stairs

### Poisonous Plants

The following plants can cause severe poisoning (this is not a complete listing):

- Aconite
- Azalea
- Foxglove
- Hemlock
- Hydrangea
- Ivy
- Larkspur
- Mistletoe
- Nightshade
- Oleander (rosebay)
- Rhododendron
- Sweet pea

The following plants cause uncomfortable, though usually not life-threatening, reactions (again, this is not a complete listing):

- Calla lily
- Daffodil bulb
- Dieffenbachia
- Holly
- Hyacinth
- Iris
- Laurel
- Philodendron
- Poinsettia
- Tomato leaves
- Wisteria
- Yellow jasmine
- Yew

## Visiting hours

Once you have childproofed everything in sight you will be faced with another problem – other people's houses. This is whole new source of trauma for parents, but try not to worry unduly and spoil the trip. It is impossible to stop a mobile baby from exploring new surroundings, but by being aware of potential dangers you can keep your child safe and enjoy your visit:

- Don't be embarrassed to discuss safety issues on visits – you are responsible for your child.
- Bring anything with you that you need to keep your baby safe, such as a high chair or playpen.
- If your friends or relatives don't have young children of their own, they are not likely to have childproofing methods in place.
- Keep an eye on any pets
- Older children often love to play with babies, but some of their toys may be unsuitable for a baby.
- Ask if doors to other rooms can be closed if your baby is liable to go exploring.

Remember: there is no substitute for supervising your baby, so be careful not to become distracted.

### Baby Walkers

Baby walkers do not help babies to walk. Besides being potentially dangerous – putting babies at risk of crashing into or reaching dangerous objects, such as a hot stove, or tumbling down stairs – they can interfere with motor development. Studies have found that babies who used walkers for two-and-a-half hours a day were delayed in walking and other motor milestones. The reason: walkers make it too easy for babies to get where they want to go, and they don't experience the frustration that spurs the development of their motor skills. Babies need to see what they are doing as they try to work out how to take their first steps. But, in many styles of walkers, babies' feet are out of sight.

## First Aid

As the parent of a small child, you'll be administering a lot of first aid – particularly once your child is getting around on her own. You can minimize the hazards by childproofing, but your baby will still get her fair share of accidents in her first year.

CAUTION: Do not use baby wipes to clean a cut. They sting and can be irritating to the damaged tissues.

### The First Aid Kit

Once your baby becomes mobile, you'll be patching up scrapes and bumps, pulling out splinters and administering other forms of first aid. You'll need:

- First aid manual
- Telephone number of doctorl
- Sterile gauze
- Steristrips or butterfly bandages
- Adhesive strip bandages
- Adhesive tape

- Antiseptic wipes
- Elastic bandage
- Tweezers
- Old credit card (to scrape bee stings)
- Calamine lotion
- Cold packs (instant, or keep one in the freezer; use a bag of frozen vegetables in a pinch)
- Cotton balls
- Scissors
- Safety pins
- Eye bath
- Antiseptic cream
- Non-adhesive sterile wound dressings

## Common Injuries

- **Burns:** Soak the burned area in cool water for at least 20 minutes or until the pain fades. You can hold the burn under cold running water or put ice and cold water in a bowl. Don't use ice alone; it can increase the damage to the skin. Do not put butter or other greases on a burn – they trap the heat and make it worse. And don't pop any blisters that develop; just cover them with a bandage. Redness and a slight swelling are signs of a first-degree burn (the least serious); blistering and significant swelling indicate a second-degree burn; areas that seem white or charred indicate a third-degree burn. If you suspect a second- or third-degree burn, see a doctor immediately.
- **Poison ingestion:** Take away the poisonous substance, if your child is still holding any, and remove any left in his mouth with your fingers. Keep anything that you remove for later analysis. If you suspect your baby has swallowed poison, call an ambulance. If he vomits, keep a sample to show the doctor, but do not force your child to be sick, as this may make the problem worse. Do not give your baby a drink, unless it's on the doctor's advice. Remember that even tiny amounts of alcohol or vitamins can poison a child.

- **Sand in the eye:** Try to keep your baby from rubbing his eye, but otherwise do nothing; tears will usually wash out the sand. If not, you can help them by washing the eye with a saline solution. If nothing you do seems to work, call your doctor.

- **Bee stings:** If the sting is visible, try to remove it by scraping across the skin with a credit card. Do not squeeze it. Wash the area with soap and water and apply an ice pack to reduce swelling. Call the doctor is your baby has a sting in the mouth or throat. If your baby has a severe reaction—swelling that extends far beyond the site of the sting, a rapid heartbeat, clammy skin, hives or trouble breathing – call an ambulance.

- **Sunburn:** If you're like most of us, your first reaction to your baby's sunburn will be guilt. 'Oh, how can I have forgotten to put lotion on? Why did we stay at the park all afternoon? Why didn't I go home when I realized I forgot his hat?' After you're finished berating yourself about this, give your baby a bath in cool water or soak some flannels in water and lay them over the burned area. When he's dry, spread aloe (100 per cent) on the burned area. Or soak your baby in a lukewarm bath with either 15g of baking soda or a cup of comfrey tea in it (comfrey reduces swelling). Give him some ibuprofen or aspirin (if there are no fever or cold symptoms). If the burn blisters, if your baby gets a fever or chills, or if he seems very ill, call the doctor.

- **Cuts:** Stop the bleeding by applying pressure directly to the cut. If the cut 'smiles' (the edges are further apart in the middle than on the ends), is deep, or may have dirt or glass stuck inside, see a doctor. Wash the cut thoroughly with soap and water, apply an antiseptic ointment, and put on a plaster. If the cut isn't particularly deep or long, it will probably stay closed on its own. Or you can bring the edges together and fasten themwith a butterfly bandage or steristrip before covering it with a regular plaster.

When your baby does get hurt, how you react will influence her reaction. If you are matter-of-fact about the injury ('Oh, you scraped your knee. Come on, let's get a plaster'), administering first aid will be a lot easier for both of you.

- **Nettle rash:** Stinging nettles produce an itchy red rash on the skin. These rashes look alarming, but are usually harmless. Dab the area with calamine lotion, or place a cold compress on the rash to relieve the itching. Dock leaves are nature's remedy for nettle rash, and normally grow near to nettles. Rub the affected area gently with the leaves to relieve the discomfort.
- **Insect bites:** These are not a major deal for most babies, and usually look worse than they feel. If your baby seems to be itching, put a facecloth wrung out in iced water on the bite. If the itching doesn't seem to stop, or the area keeps swelling, call your doctor, who may prescribe an antihistamine.
- **Scrapes:** Run cold water over the scrape and wash it with soap. Pat it dry with a clean cloth, dab it with antiseptic cream, and bandage it . Go to the doctor if the scrape is deep, bleeding heavily or embedded with gravel or dirt, or if you see more redness or pus.

## Choking

If your baby seems to be choking, first lay him face down along your forearm, supporting his head and neck, and slap him on the back five times between the shoulder blades. Put your finger into his mouth and feel for any obstructions. However, do NOT feel down his throat. If this doesn't work, turn the baby onto his back and placing two fingers on the lower half of his breastbone, give five sharp downward thrusts – one every three seconds – then check his mouth for obstruction again. If this does not work, take your baby with you while you call for an ambulance, but repeat the cycle of back slaps and chest thrusts while you wait. Do not use the Heimlich manoeuvre: a baby's bones and organs are too fragile

# A & E

Sometimes a kiss, a plaster and an ice pack aren't enough. The following injuries may require immediate medical attention:

**Head injuries:**
- The bleeding doesn't stop after ten minutes of direct pressure
- He cries for more than ten minutes
- A severe fall (down the stairs, for example)
- He has a seizure
- He was unconscious, no matter how briefly
- He vomits more than twice
- His pupils are unequal in size
- His eyes are crossed

**Cuts:** Very deep or present a 'smile' (the skin edges in the centre of the cut are wider apart than on the ends.

**Burns:** Have blistering, significant swelling, while patches or charring.

CHAPTER 17

# Travels with Baby

Babies are portable. They are easy to carry, will sleep just about anywhere, and don't beg to stop at for fast food. Take advantage of this while you can, and take your baby on the road. Go out every day; your baby will thrive on exposure to new sights, sounds and smells, and you'll keep yourself from going mad. You won't be this mobile again for years to come.

## Getting Around Town

Babies don't much care where they're going when they go out, but mums tend to feel a little aimless without a destination. When my first son was a newborn, I got into the habit of buying stamps one at a time, because the post office was an easy walk from my house. In those early days of sleep deprivation, the post office was about as far as my imagination would take me. Later, I realized how crazy this was and started finding more interesting things to do in my neighbourhood. There are several destinations available to most of us only a walk or short drive away.

Shops are great places to take babies. Grocery shops, furniture shops and bookshops are all filled with brightly coloured objects of various shapes, and people who love to smile at babies. Doors designed for wheelchair access are also buggy-friendly.

Go grocery shopping. Your infant car seat may be designed to clip safely to the seat of a shopping trolley, or you can place it inside. Perhaps your local supermarket has special trolleys with built-in infant seats. (You may want to clean the seat with a baby wipe.) You can also shop with your baby in a frontpack or sling or leave him in his buggy.

Supermarkets sometimes give free helium balloons to children. Tie one to the car seat, trolley or buggy for instant entertainment. If your baby is eating finger foods, try the free samples, or ask for a slice of a soft fruit.

Go to a shoopping centre. Talk to your baby about all the things you see. Admire the fountains, and window-shop. (You don't have to actually buy anything.) I was never more up-to-date on fashion trends than during my maternity leaves.

Stay away from clothing shops with narrow aisles and tightly-packed racks. Your baby will end up with his face shoved into clothes, breathing chemicals (used to protect the fabric), gnawing on tags and dribbling on something you can't throw in the washer.

Shops also get bonus points as a parent/baby destination because they often have clean toilets – some, in upmarket department stores, border on the luxurious. (On one particularly memorable outing I took with a bunch of mums, some of them with infants, we stopped at a department store toilet out of necessity. We settled in a couch for a few extra moments so one mum could nurse her baby, and ended up staying for more than an hour, lulled by the fresh flowers and soft music.)

## See the Sights

Consider spending a day at a museum. Ring ahead and confirm that the museum you are considering visiting allows a baby backpack or a buggy. (Some don't at all, some do on certain days.) Frontpacks and slings can pretty well go anywhere. When your baby is ready to eat, pick a bench in front of a painting you really like; if you're nursing, swap paintings when you swap breasts.

Be a tourist in your own town. Big or small, your town probably has some tourist destinations locals are usually too busy to visit. If you live in a city, you probably already have your favourite spots to take visitors. Revisit them, and discover a few more.

# Gear Up for Travelling

Just as you prepared your home for an infant, and can look forward to a whole new set of gizmos and gadgets for childproofing, travels with baby require very specific equipment. Do some research. Ask other new mums or your paediatrician for their recommendations.

## The Equipment

- **Car seat:** Car seat models, I'm told, expire after six years, and technology is constantly changing. Make sure yours is up to date and appropriate for your model of car. it is also vital that the seat is correctly installed – ask your garage for help if need be. Remember: you will not be able to take your baby home from hospital by car without a suitable car seat.
- **Buggy:** Buggies for infants should fully recline. If yours doesn't, borrow one that does or use a metal frame that converts your car seat into a buggy until your baby can sit upright without slumping.

- **Jogging or off-road buggy:** A luxury item, unless you're a regular runner, but far easier to push on and off pavements when you're out for a long walk.
- **Rain cover for your buggy**
- **Sling and/or frontpack**
- **Baby backpack:** Once your baby can sit supported, these are better for long walks with a heavy baby than a frontpack.
- **Nappy bag or nappy backpack**
- **Portable crib or playpen:** Hotels (and sometimes grandparents) will often supply cribs upon request, but these aren't usually in the best condition. If you use one, measure the slats – they shouldn't be more than 60mm (2 ⅜in) apart. If your baby isn't too mobile, you can put a dresser drawer on the floor and line it with a folded towel or two. Or bring a child's paddling pool (it fold up small and inflates easily; make sure it's firm when inflated), and line it with a towel or blanket. If you're in a family bed, you don't need anything.
- **Portable highchair:** If your baby is eating finger foods, a highchair will make mealtimes a lot more pleasant for everyone. We found that a clip-on highchair fitted in the bottom of our biggest duffel bag.
- **Bike seat or bike trailer, and helmet**

## The Accessories

The more comprehensive your nappy bag, the less you'll end up buying on the road. Use your judgement, however. If the majority of your trips are to run errands or pick up older siblings, you may not need everything on this list. Pack the less-used items in a separate bag to keep with you for day trips and overnight stays. Pack in advance to prevent last-minute rushing – that's when you forget the essentials.

- ❏ Nappies (at least four)
- ❏ Refillable pack of baby wipes
- ❏ Nappy rash ointment
- ❏ Plastic bags
- ❏ Light blanket (to cover your baby or use as a play mat)
- ❏ Waterproof changing pad or rubberized sheet

- ❏ Terry nappy (for burping and general cleaning up)
- ❏ Sunscreen (for babies over six months)
- ❏ Bottles and formula, unless you're nursing exclusively
- ❏ Food for your older baby (oat rings, etc.)
- ❏ Snack for yourself
- ❏ Water bottle (for Mum to drink, for cleaning up)
- ❏ Change of clothes for your baby
- ❏ Extra shirt for yourself
- ❏ Stain remover stick
- ❏ Travel pack of tissues
- ❏ A few toys or rattles
- ❏ Paperback book or magazine for Mum
- ❏ Mobile phone

# Dining Out

Take yourself out to lunch, breakfast or dinner as often as you can when your baby is in the 'luggage' stage (i.e. you can set her down anywhere and she doesn't move). Until your baby is eating solids, you don't even have to worry about selecting a child-friendly restaurant. You actually can eat at a restaurant that has tablecloths (but go early, it'll be less crazy and more fun). Become a regular at a favourite restaurant; you may find your baby 'adopted' by the staff, who greet her by name. If your baby is sleeping in her car seat, you may be able to safely tuck her under the table for a while. If your baby is hungry and you're nursing, toss a napkin over your shoulder and settle her in to feed; just order a meal that's not too hard to eat with one hand – and avoid hot soup or coffee.

## Choose a Child-Friendly Restaurant

Once your child can join you in a meal, pick a restaurant that caters for families. If your child is noisy, the other diners won't care as much, since you won't be interrupting romantic meals. The restaurant staff will be used to spills, and the other children around will entertain your baby.

## Top Ten Signs You've Found a Family Restaurant

10. The tablecloths are really paper.
9. Your entrance went unremarked by the other diners, and the people seated at tables near the door didn't turn around and stare.
8. Your child immediately sniffs out a toy box or play area.
7. The waiters don't look worried or panicked when you struggle in, loaded down with baby and gear.
6. Helium balloons are tied to the salad bar.
5. It's just noisy enough so you can't hear a spoon drop.
4. You see several families with kids and a big mess.
3. The waiter automatically picks up colouring sheets and crayons before leading you to your table.
2. More than one highchair is in plain view.
1. You don't need to make a special request for a children's menu.

### Other Tips

- Bring finger foods, and dole them out slowly
- Bring a few small toys in case the finger foods lose their appeal
- Place your order as quickly as you can, and when the food arrives, ask for the bill (you may make it through dinner with a contented baby, only to have him melt down during a long wait for the bill)
- Forget about coffee and dessert – if you make it through a salad and main course, consider yourself lucky
- Tip as much as you can; you'll be remembered for that, instead of the mess you left in your wake

## Feeding an Older Baby

If you didn't pack dinner for your older baby, take a creative look at the menu. Do the main courses come with vegetables? Maybe you can get a side dish of steamed vegetables and cut them small or mash them. (It may take the kitchen two tries to cook the vegetables soft enough for a baby.) Are there eggs on the menu? Ask for scrambled eggs, yolks only. Is there a salad bar? Scavenge it for soft fruits and vegetables you can cut into bite-sized pieces. Are you in a Chinese, Japanese or Thai restaurant? Ask for a dish of cold tofu with a dash of soy sauce. An

Italian restaurant? Try a dish of polenta or risotto. And most chefs can quickly prepare a dish of plain pasta.

## Two Thumbs Up

Go to the cinema. Catch an afternoon matinee, when cinemas are nearly empty, or an evening show on a weeknight. Pick an aisle seat, just in case you need to bolt – but the odds are that you won't. Cinemas are dark, and after nursing or drinking a bottle, your baby is likely to go to sleep. If not, she may relax and watch the show. Or bring quiet cloth toys and teething rings (leave the rattles at home). This is not, however, the time to pick an action movie that amplifies tyre squeals and gunshots in full digital surround sound. Go for a 'chick flick' with lots of dialogue and close-ups of faces (which babies love). My youngest was a regular at my monthly cinema group until he was nearly ten months old.

## Hit the Trail

If you like to walk, you don't have to give it up now; if you never were a walker, this may be the time to start (but begin with short, easy routes). Stay out of constant sun (don't forget your baby's hat), and avoid paths with low branches. Use a frontpack until your baby is too heavy for one, then switch to a backpack.

Or just walk around town. Admire your neighbours' gardens; get to know the neighbourhood pets by name. Don't limit your walks to balmy spring days. Try rain walks. If your baby is in a frontpack, sling or backpack, an umbrella will protect both of you, and your baby will be fascinated by the sound and smell of rain. Go out for an evening walk and bring a torch for extra baby entertainment.

What about parks and playgrounds? They're a great place to meet other mums, but save them for after your baby is sitting or crawling and can take advantage of the swings and sandpit. Until then, pick outings that interest you more; you'll be getting plenty of playground time over the next few years.

## Biker Baby

After your baby is able to hold up and control her head for extended periods of time (usually at around nine months), she's ready to experience life in the bike lane. Get a helmet that fits her well (make sure it has a gently rounded, not flared, back, or she won't be able to lean her head back comfortably) and a bike seat (make sure the seat keeps her feet away from the wheels) or a trailer.

# Road Warrior

Some babies seem to fall asleep the minute they feel the car's motor start; others scream. Cecily's baby Henry fell into the former category, so she did a lot of errands by car to get her often-fretful baby to sleep. My babies fell into the latter category, at least until they put on enough weight to travel in forward-facing car seats.

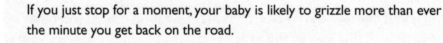

If you just stop for a moment, your baby is likely to grizzle more than ever the minute you get back on the road.

The problem with car travel for some babies seems to be boredom. For a very young baby, pictures to look at may help. Prop a book or a plastic picture holder designed for the car on the seat facing your baby; or try hanging a mirror designed for crib use from the back headrest so your baby can admire herself. Company in the back seat or music also keep your baby content. Bring toys for older babies; hook them to the car seat with plastic links, or they'll all end up on the floor in minutes. Stopping – to change a nappy or soothe the baby – usually doesn't help, unless you're planning a long stop.

## Packing for Holidays

In addition to clothes for your baby, you'll need:

- ❏ Car seat
- ❏ Buggy
- ❏ Food for trip, including powdered formula and water, if you're bottle-feeding
- ❏ Nappies and wipes (bring enough for two days; buy the rest at your destination)
- ❏ A favourite toy
- ❏ 'New' toy for trip
- ❏ Lovey, if she has one
- ❏ Portable crib, sheets, favourite blanket
- ❏ Portable highchair
- ❏ Tapes or CDs of music if you're travelling by car
- ❏ Babyproofing gadgets (If your baby is crawling, babyproof at least one room at your destination, or it won't be much of a break for you. Bring a pack of socket covers and a few cabinet locks.)
- ❏ Your doctor's phone number
- ❏ First aid kit
- ❏ Sticky tape (endless, nondestructive entertainment)
- ❏ Sunblock

## Your Itinerary

If you're going on a long trip, try to plan the trip around your baby's regular sleep schedule. For instance, she might be happily awake in the car seat for as much as an hour – but not much more. If you leave an hour before nap time, she'll be awake for an hour and fall asleep, if you're lucky, for two hours. Then stop to feed her, change her, maybe eat dinner yourself, and get her back in the car for another hour awake and hope that brings you to your destination.

If your baby is hungry, don't remove her from her car seat while the car is in motion. Stop to nurse. (One mum reports leaning over her baby's car seat from the adjoining seat without undoing her own seatbelt, but doesn't recommend it for others. 'I will never take a long road trip with a child that small again,' she said.)

The best news about car travel is that children under the age of two rarely suffer from travel sickness. This particular treat may be in your future, but is not something you have to deal with right now.

## The Not-So-Friendly Skies

There is nothing that instils panic in the minds of parents – as well as other passengers and flight attendants – as the thought of a baby's first aeroplane trip. It can be rough. Actually, it can be horrible. Your baby may scream for hours, throw up all over you and leak through his last dry set of clothes (been there, done that, and wouldn't even talk about getting on a plane for the next six months). Or your baby may sleep the whole way, and wake only as the plane is coming in for a landing.

When planning trips that include your baby, try to make plane reservations for his *least* fretful time of day.

While travelling with an infant may be rough on parents, it isn't, under normal circumstances, hazardous to the baby. There is no clear medical reason to forego air travel until an infant is a certain age, although some airlines have restrictions on travel for infants only a few days old. Unless a trip is critical, you might consider not going until your baby is more than two months old; aeroplanes tend to be germ-rich places, and when a baby under two months old gets a fever for any reason, it is a concern.

To some extent, whether you spend your flight reading a novel or passing out earplugs is a combination of your baby's temperament and luck. But you can beat the odds.

When you make your reservations, think about your child's temperament at different times of the day. If he is fretful every evening and needs to be walked for hours, a late-day flight is probably not a good idea. If he typically falls asleep easily and sleeps all night, maybe you're a candidate for a night flight. (This is a risky move, though: fellow passengers, who will grin and bear it when a baby is crying on a daytime flight, can get downright nasty when their night's sleep is interrupted by a crying baby.)

## A Seat of One's Own

Consider purchasing a seat for your baby. Yes, he can fly free (or, on international flights, for a small fee), and the extra cost may be prohibitive, but having a guaranteed spot for your baby's car seat can make the difference between a merely stressful flight and torture. (You can put him down if he falls asleep, for one, and be able to lower your tray table and eat something yourself.) It's also a lot safer. Ask – it probably won't cost as much as your ticket and many carriers have greatly reduced fares for children under two.

If you do purchase a seat, make sure to reserve the window for your baby; you won't be allowed to use the car seat in any other seat, as it may block access to the aisle. You can also request a baby meal. Most airlines offer this option, which is usually a few jars of baby food.

## Know What to Ask For

If you aren't purchasing an extra seat and are travelling with another adult or child, ask for an aisle and a window seat when you make your reservations. If you're lucky, the centre seat will remain unoccupied. If not, whoever is assigned that seat will be happy to swap for your aisle or window seat and may, if your baby starts fretting before take-off, look for a seat far away. (Hint: boarding is not the time to worry about quietening your baby; you *want* to clear your row.) You may have been advised to ask for a bulkhead row. This tip makes sense, but unless you or your travelling companion are a high-mileage flier, forget about it; most airlines award bulkhead seats to good customers, not families with kids.

Try to get a seat in the front third of the airplane. Some planes have been remodelled to give front passengers extra leg room, and those few centimetres may make the difference between whether you can wriggle down to pick up a dropped rattle or not. If the front third is booked, try for one of the last few rows. You'll be close to the toilet and at least have some floor space to pace with your baby.

## Travel Tips

- **Gate-check your buggy.** Tell the person checking boarding passes that you want a gate-check; he'll give you a special tag. Then you can push your baby all the way down the boarding ramp and unload your buggy just outside the door to the airplane. Put on the tag and leave the buggy there. It will be returned to you as you leave the airplane at your destination and will make it a lot easier to get your baby and her gear to the baggage area.

- **Bring a car seat aboard.** (Make sure that it's no wider than fifteen inches—that means it will fit in most coach seats.) You may also have to prove that your car seat is FAA-approved; if it doesn't say so on the label, it may in the instruction manual. Some infant seats fit in the overhead compartment; if yours does, and you don't have a seat reserved for your baby, stash it there as soon as you get it on the plane. You can get it down later if it turns out you have an extra seat. If it doesn't fit, and the plane is full, you'll have to ask the flight attendant to check it for you. If you are using a convertible car seat (the kind that can be strapped in the rear-facing position for infants and switched to front-facing for older children), you may have to strap it in the front-facing position to fit it on the plane. This isn't ideal, but it's safer than your lap.

- **Bring plenty of extra formula.** Plane travel is dehydrating, and sucking will help protect your baby's ears from pressure problems. If you're using powdered formula, bring plenty of water. (I'll never forget the time I asked a flight attendant repeatedly for water for my son's bottle, and was eventually shooed over to the bathroom and told to help myself at the tap. I did, and was shaking the bottle to mix the formula when I noticed the label above the sink: 'Not drinking water'.)

- **Pre-boarding.** It's easier to get yourself and your gear stowed, strapped in and settled before hordes of anxious passengers are trying to cram past you. Unfortunately, this courtesy is offered less and less often. If there isn't an announcement, ask if you can pre-board; some airlines will respond to individual requests. If you're traveling as a solo parent with a baby, beg. Grovelling is better than being trampled by impatient passengers as you are trying to stow your gear without dropping your baby.

- **Nurse or feed your baby during take-off and landing.** The sucking and swallowing helps prevent discomfort in her ears from the changes in air pressure. If she's sleeping during take-off, let her sleep; but if she's sleeping during landing, wake her up, as that's when the pressure problems are the worst. If she's not interested in eating, use an eyedropper to put drops of water, juice or milk in her mouth. She'll swallow them, and the swallowing will clear her ears. (Screaming will clear her ears too, of course.)

- **Drink plenty of fluids yourself.** (Bring a sports water bottle, and get it refilled; it's easier to manage while wrestling a baby than a plastic glass or drinks can.) This is critical if you are nursing. Again, air travel is extremely dehydrating. If you're not careful, your milk supply can be depleted for a day or two.

- **Bring extra clothes.** Your baby is not the only one who is going to get messy if he throws up or has a nappy blow-out. Keep a change of clothes (for yourself) and plastic grocery bags (for the mess) in your hand luggage.

- **Bring a favourite toy or two.** Be on the lookout for found toys too. (The laminated card with the picture of emergency exits somehow fascinates babies; you can make puppets out of sick bags or play stacking games with paper cups from the toilet.)

- **Bring a packet of disposable earplugs.** If your baby's screaming is getting you a lot of nasty looks from nearby passengers, stand up and offer the earplugs around. You'll at least get a laugh, which may win a few people over to your side.

If you'd like a more peaceful baby when flying, try a bottle of chamomile tea. (My breast-feeding babies, who never wanted anything to do with bottles of breast milk or formula, were usually willing to drink this on an aeroplane.) Brew it before you leave, adding a teaspoon of sugar to about three-quarters of a cup of hot tea, and pour it into a bottle. It'll be lukewarm when you're on board.

## Other Travel Challenges

One fiction that you need to drop is the idea that the flight attendant is your friend. She may have been your friend when you were travelling on business, carrying a jacket and a briefcase, and quietly sitting in your aisle seat, tapping away on your computer. She is probably not your friend when you are pacing the aisle, trying to calm your screaming baby while simultaneously dodging the drinks trolley. Once in a while, you'll get a wonderful flight attendant who has – or remembers what it is like to have – young children. If the flight isn't too crowded, the attendant may volunteer to hold your baby while you go to the toilet. (Those of us who have met those flight attendants remember them forever.) The odds are, however, that you won't; you'll be on your own.

Finding a place to change a nappy on a plane is a challenge. Forget about the toilets. Only rarely will you get a plane with a fold-down changing table, and the ones that exist are so small as to be practically useless. The toilets themselves have no counter space, and the floors are typically wet and sticky.

If you have a row to yourself, change your baby on your seats. Smile apologetically to nearby passengers if it's a smelly nappy, and whisk it into the asick bag as quickly as possible. Speed is important here.

If you don't have a row to yourself, your best bet is to change your baby on the floor at the back of the plane. Try to crouch out of the path of anyone who might walk by, and put a blanket or two on the floor before you spread out your changing pad (again, the floor is likely to be pretty yucky). Alternatively, try to dodge the issue by lathering your baby's bottom with nappy cream and putting a superabsorbent nappy or double-nappies on him just before boarding, and hope he doesn't poo before landing.

If you're switching planes as a solo parent and can't figure out how you are going to race with your baby, car seat and nappy bag from gate to gate, try calling the airline. You may be able to arrange for help in the form of a chauffeured electric cart. Or, if you're desperate, request a wheelchair. (OK, I've never tried this, and the airlines are going to hate me for suggesting it. But it has been done. And I had my easiest plane trip with an infant when I had my leg in a cast. The baby and luggage rode on my lap as I was rolled to the gate. I was pre-boarded without a fuss, and assigned one of those prime bulkhead seats.)

## International Baby

All children must have their own individual passport – even newborns. This passport will need to be signed by a parent or someone with parental responsibility. Each application must be supported by two photographs, 45 x 35mm (1¾ x 1⅜in), taken against a light-coloured background. These photos must be identical and show the child's full face.

Obviously, providing a photograph of a young baby presents something of a challenge. The passport agency will not accept photographs with the parent in as well as the baby, however, for young babies it is acceptable to have a hand in the picture supporting the baby's head. Remember that passport photos do not have to come from a booth, so going to a professional photographer may offer a convenient alternative to battling with a photo booth. A child's passport is valid for five years, but as young children change dramatically, you will have to plan ahead before taking your child on an overseas trip and renew the passport for your child if necessary.

Make sure you tell the travel company when you book that you will be travelling with a baby. Many airlines will offer seats with extra legroom to parents with infants, but these are limited so it's strictly first-come-first-served. Check with the airline whether you will be able to take a pushchair right up to the departure gate. Many travel companies will offer help where they can as long as you tell them in advance.

If you are packing baby formula, make sure it is unopened. (Pack formula for the plane ride separately). Otherwise, you may not be able to bring it into the country. Be sure to declare it, if asked.

# Feeling Adventurous?

## To the Woods

You can go camping with an infant, although you may have to pack a few more things than you are used to. Along with your regular camping gear, consider bringing:

- A waterproof crib pad for inside your sleeping bag, if you're sleeping with your baby
- A portable crib, if you're not
- An inflatable paddling pool for use as bathtub and/or crib
- A large plastic bin to pack your clothes in and use as a tub to wash your baby
- An extra-warm babygrow
- A blanket for sitting on when you are outside the tent
- A highchair if your baby is eating finger foods (it will give him a chance to get the food in his mouth before it gets covered with dirt, and can be used to contain him when you don't want to worry about him crawling into the fire)

Check your campsite completely before letting your baby loose, in case previous campers left things behind that you'd don't want your baby to put in his mouth.

## Beach Baby

I'm a beach person, so the first place I think of taking an infant on holiday is a tropical beach. All three of my kids were in the water before they could crawl, and took long afternoon naps under beach umbrellas.

'I went to the beach a lot when my kids were infants,' said Alissa. 'All you really need is an umbrella and a good chair to support yourself while you are nursing.'

If you are planning a day or longer at the beach with your baby, be sure to protect her from the sun. (While chemical sunblocks don't seem to have any negative effects on young babies, you may want to try one that uses zinc or titanium oxide, which provides physical rather than chemical blocks.) Patch-test any sunblock before covering your baby with it. (Put a dab on the inside of your baby's arm and cover it with a bandage. Check the skin after 20 minutes, and again after 24 hours. You're looking for red blotches or bumps. If you see them, cross that brand off your list.)

Also:

- Whether or not you are using sunblock, dress your baby in lightweight cotton clothes that cover her arms and legs. Use a hat, with a brim that goes all the way around, and sunglasses. She may not keep them on, but she may love them. If she does, you'll be protecting her from long-term eye damage and short-term fretting – bright sun glaring off water may make her uncomfortable. You can also invest in special UV clothes that are lightweight and sunproof, even when wet.
- Bring or hire an umbrella and keep her in the shade as much as possible. Consider getting off the beach altogether in the middle of the day, when the sun is at its highest and hottest.
- If she's old enough to hang onto a toy, bring a bucket and spade. She may not know how to play with them yet, but she'll love it when you demonstrate water dumping and castle building. (Her job at this point is to knock your castles down.)
- Bring lots of regular nappies or swim nappies. (Swim nappies pull on like training pants and, because they don't contain the superabsorbent gels of regular nappies, won't immediately fill up with water and explode. They contain poo pretty well, but do less well with pee.) Too much time in a wet nappy can start a bout of nappy rash, so you will need to change your baby often.

Always keep small plastic grocery bags with you. They are perfect for collecting (and properly disposing of) dirty nappies and used wipes.

- Bring extra T-shirts. Leave a shirt on when your baby is splashing in the water to protect him from the sun, and change it when he's out.
- Bring (and remember to drink) extra fluids, so you and your baby stay properly hydrated.
- Use cornflour or cornflour-based baby powder to remove sand—it works better than water.

While you'll want to dip your baby's toes in the water, don't take her all the way into the sea or a pool until she can support her head on her own. The water temperature ought to be fairly warm – above 28.8°C (84°F) to prevent hypothermia. You shouldn't keep your baby in the water longer than half an hour; even water that warm will eventually chill your child.

In a pool, go ahead and use a rubber ring specially designed for a baby (with straps between the legs) or a life jacket, but don't consider these as replacements for your arms – stay within reach. A baby can slip from a ring, or tip face-first into the water when wearing a jacket.

## A Potpourri of Travel Tips

*Take that big holiday* before your child is crawling or eating solid foods – it will be your last 'easy' family holiday for a long time.

*If you're walking* with your baby in a backpack, carry a make-up mirror in your pocket. Pull it out to use as a rear-view mirror to check on your baby.

*For bottle-feeding* on a short outing, fill a bottle with hot water before you leave, wrap it in a small towel, then tuck it into a foam tin-holder. The water will stay warm for hours; just add premeasured powdered formula when you're ready to feed your baby.

*Eating in a restaurant?* Leave a tip commensurate with the size of the mess you're leaving behind.

*Camping?* If you're not nursing and your baby needs a middle-of-the-night feed, tuck a tin of premixed formula into your sleeping bag; it will be warm when your baby wakes up hungry.

*To warm a bottle* on an aeroplane, fill an asick bag halfway with hot water (the flight attendants will have the water available for tea). Put the bottle in the water and let it sit.

*If you're staying in a hotel* with a minibar, lock it. If it doesn't lock, ask for it to be emptied.

*When checking into a hotel,* mention that your baby wakes at night. You'll probably then be assigned to a room with vacancies around it, or at the end of a hall, and you'll be less likely to disturb other guests.

*Struggling with a fussy baby on an aeroplane?* Let Dad handle it; your baby may fuss just as much, but Dad is likely to get more sympathetic looks from the other passengers and help (and sometimes free drinks, as mums report) from the flight attendants. (Sexist, but true.)

*If you can afford it,* buy a separate aeroplane ticket for your baby. Having that extra seat, with a car seat strapped into it, is safer for your baby, and for you can make the difference between a tolerable trip and a torturous one.

*Wooden highchairs,* available in some restaurants, invert to make stable stands for an infant seat. (Check to make sure that the seat is indeed stable before resting it there.)

CHAPTER 18

# Time for Yourself

n the weeks that follow the birth of your baby, the initially constant flow of blood will slow to a trickle and then stop. Your breasts will adjust to nursing – or not nursing – and will cease to feel like foreign objects suddenly attached to your body. You may not be getting much sleep, but you'll get used to surviving on whatever sleep you do get.

## Life Postpartum

Tearful, overwhelmed and strange *is* normal in the postpartum weeks – and sometimes months. You may be irritable and sometimes angry. You may have dramatic mood swings. You may shed tears for no explicable reason, and may find yourself unable to cope with situations you would normally handle with ease. You may blow up in anger when those around you least expect it.

Get a flu jab. Maybe you're not in an official at-risk group, but do you really think you can handle the demands of being a new mother *and* a bout with the flu?

This is normal. It is normal to have an emotional reaction to a major life change – and a new baby *is* a major life change. It is normal to be stressed by the demands placed on you as a new mother, to be daunted by the responsibility that is suddenly, literally, in your lap. It is normal to be exhausted when your sleep is constantly interrupted. And it is normal to have a host of physical and emotional reactions to the dramatic postpartum change in your hormone levels. The rapid drop in oestrogen levels causes hot flushes, depression and trouble concentrating. (So you really need a preview of menopause at this point!) The drop in progesterone can cause anxiety (progesterone, in high doses, has sometimes been prescribed to relieve anxiety). The fall in the level of thyroid function can make you feel sluggish. Mood-controlling hormones, such as serotonin and dopamine, drop as well.

## What You Can Do

If you feel like you're out of control, you are. It's not because you can't handle being a mum – it's pure biochemistry. It will probably pass on its own, although you may not believe it at the time. This feeling may be normal, but you don't have to sit there and wait for it to go away. Take a nap or get some exercise. Go outside - sunlight helps. Eat regularly and well. (If you're a stay-at-home mum, pack yourself a lunch in the morning before your partner leaves, or you may miss lunch altogether.) Drink liquids constantly – you need extra for breast-feeding, and fatigue can be a symptom of dehydration. Ask for help from family or friends. (My favourite break was to hand the baby to my husband after dinner and get in the bathtub. Sometimes my bath lasted for hours.) Hire a babysitter for a few hours. If you're falling apart and can't get a break immediately, try breast-feeding for a while – the released hormones may be just enough to relax you.

For some women, the hormonal changes may be too extreme to handle without a doctor's help and/or medication. If you fit into that category, you're not a wimp; you're just chemically out of synch.

## Depression Statistics

If you're feeling overemotional, overwhelmed and possibly depressed, you are not alone. Consider these statistics:

- At least 50 per cent of new mothers experience at least a short-term case of the baby blues.
- 10–15 per cent of mothers become clinically depressed in the first year after the birth of a child.
- Two in 1,000 new mothers develop postpartum psychosis, which goes beyond depression to hallucinations and delusions, and, sometimes, violent behaviour.

## Baby Blues Checklist

'I see it coming when a mother is constantly tired and crying,' says midwife Jean Rasch. 'She isn't enjoying her baby, she hates her partner, and she isn't sleeping. She worries every time she has to deal with the baby – that she didn't get any sleep when he took his last nap; that she won't get any sleep when he takes his next one. And she is really different – chemically different. She is acting different to the way I know her, to the way her partner knows her.'

## Post Natal Depression

The symptoms of post natal depression (PND) usually reveal themselves in the first few months after the birth, but may originate from pregnancy or even before. Although all new mothers fall prey to exhaustion, anxiety and lack of confidence, a mother suffering from post natal depression may experience a combination of symptoms.

- Lethargy.
- Tearfulness.
- Anxiety.
- Guilt.
- Irritability.
- Confusion.
- Disturbed sleep.
- Excessive exhaustion.
- Difficulties making decisions.
- Loss of self-esteem.
- Lack of confidence in her ability as a mother.
- No enjoyment of motherhood.
- Fear of harming herself or the baby*.
- Loss of appetite.
- Hostility or indifference to people she normally loves.
- Difficulty in concentrating.
- Shame at being unable to be happy.
- Fear of judgement.
- Helplessness.

(data supplied by the Natural Childbirth Trust)

*If you are having suicidal thoughts or thoughts about harming your baby, tell your doctor or a trusted friend immediately.

If you are experiencing an increasing number of these symptoms, and they intensify with time, make sure you get all the help you need. Tell the people in your life who are most likely to take action to get you some relief. Include at least one relative or close friend and one healthcare provider, and enlist some support sooner than later.

## Professional Help

Only one in several hundred women face postpartum problems that require medication, but if you think you are one of them, get help fast, because the disease can threaten your life – or that of your baby. Severe postpartum reactions may include depression that goes on for days at a time and gets in the way of your life; mania, including hyperactivity, sleeplessness and extreme irritability; anxiety, characterized by constant worrying or panic attacks, shortness of breath or dizziness; or psychosis, in which a mother becomes completely out of touch with reality.

Better safe than sorry! Do not be afraid to seek professional help. If you feel more comfortable with a friend, ask her to accompany you.

In the weeks after the birth, between one and two new mothers in every thousand experiences pueperal psychosis. The mother often experiences delusions, and the condition will be apparent to those around her. Many women are able to hide symptoms of post natal depression from loved ones and health professionals, but pueperal psychosis is impossible to hide.

## Just for Dads

Coping with postnatal depression can be very hard for the mother, but it is equally challenging for those around her, especially fathers and other children. If your partner has been diagnosed with PND or is experiencing any of the symptoms listed opposite it is important to give her all the support you can.

Be as sensitive as you can to her feelings and needs – sometimes she may need a break from the baby and time to herself, or she may need time alone with the baby away from other cares and concerns. So ask what she needs, and give it when you can.

If she is worried about coping find someone to be with her or give hands-on help, especially once you have gone back to work.

Give her time and space to express what she is feeling, and don't try to 'snap her out of it'. Being told that many people are worse off than her and that she is very lucky to have her beautiful baby is not helpful, and will only make her feel even more guilty than she already does.

Don't push her into doing things she really doesn't want to. Getting out and seeing friends may do her the power of good, but it may not – so let her decide. Too much cajoling can feel like bullying, and remember, she's still an adult who knows her own mind.

Don't fuss about things that don't matter. So what if you had to eat a ready-meal for the fourth time this week and she wasn't dressed when you got home? The world is not going to end as a result, and spending time caring for your baby is more important than cooking or looking like Nigella Lawson.

You may think that doing everything yourself is the answer, but watching someone else breezing through your chores can make you feel like a failure, so don't just charge in and take over. There's no need to turn yourself into Superman, you'll only end up tired and resentful, especially if you don't get the thanks you expect. Just communicate with your partner and help with what you can.

Admit that looking after a baby and recovering from giving birth are hard, and listen to her cares and concerns. She needs your emotional support more than a spotless bathroom. Someone else can clean the house and cook the dinner, but only you are her partner and the baby's father, so fulfil the role only you can fill and get help with the rest.

## About Sex

You will probably be told to refrain from having sex until after your six-week check-up. There is nothing magical about six weeks, really. If you had a vaginal delivery, you can safely have intercourse any time after all bleeding stops (bleeding indicates that your cervix is still open and bacteria could easily invade), usually in two or three weeks – if you want to, that is.

And you may want to. Not that I've actually ever met anyone who did want to, but these women are rumoured to exist, particularly among those who had easy births and babies who sleep a lot.

However, you may not want to. Your vaginal area may still be tender, your scar from any episiotomy or tearing may be sensitive. You might feel just fine physically, but the memory of how much the birth hurt may still make you cringe. Your body may feel odd when you are touched, in part because the hormonal effects of breast-feeding change your skin (this can be remedied with lotion or massage oil), and also because you're being touched so much by your baby you just can't take any more.

## Starting Again

'I remember the first time we had a babysitter was when Hanna was four weeks old. We went to a lavish affair at an expensive London hotel. We parked, went in and had some hors d'oeuvres,' Julie said. 'When we called to check on Hanna, the babysitter said she'd already drank all the breast milk I had pumped for her. We left before dinner was served and still had to pay for parking. The next time we had a babysitter, we shopped for food, AND WE THOUGHT IT WAS FUN!"

### So? What's It Like?

'It's like losing your virginity again.' – Esther

'We waited about eight weeks because I was terrified it would hurt. I turned out to be a little sensitive, but it was not the excruciating experience I had thought it would be.' – Natasha

'We waited a lot longer than six weeks, more like five to six months. When we finally did, it was, "Wow, I'd forgotten how much fun this was!" – Julie

'I was eager to do it for the intimacy, but for many months it hurt every time. My midwife wasn't very understanding; at my six-week check-up she told me I was healed and ready to go. I don't think she really believed that it hurt.' – Jenny

'Having sex after the birth was a much bigger priority for my husband than for me. For some inexplicable reason, he was turned on by the whole motherhood/nursing thing and had a hard time waiting six weeks. I could easily have waited longer.' – Cecily

## OK, Now the Truth

Some time (possibly after quite some time, particularly, research shows, if your baby wakes frequently at night), you may find yourself having fond memories of sex, fond enough to contemplate having it again, in spite of your exhaustion. Or, more likely, you may want to try it just once, to reassure yourself that everything still works, and then have no interest again for months. When you hit this point, think lubrication. Breast-feeding can cause vaginal dryness, so if this is a problem for you, buy a lubricant or ask your doctor about oestrogen creams.

**Even with a lubricant, you may find that intercourse hurts.**

Sure, you'll find articles saying that all you need to solve the lubrication problem is a little extra time for foreplay, starting with dinner out and a bottle of wine. If you're nursing, you really shouldn't have more than a little bit of wine, and in the brief hours your baby gives you between feedings, and considering how tired you probably are, how realistic is dedicating hours to foreplay? So I repeat: lubricant.

'My doctor recommended lubricant,' Sheila said. 'It did help with our lovemaking, and its name amused my husband. Whatever works!'

'We tried at six weeks,' said one mum. 'It didn't work. Than we tried again at two months, at three months and four months, but I had torn really badly at the birth and was a mass of scar tissue. Finally, after four and a half months, with the help of lots of lubricant, it worked – sort of. But I tore and bled. And my daughter was ten months old before I could have sex without intense pain.'

If it hurts, a different position may help. Consider one that puts the least amount of pressure on the scar where you tore or had an episiotomy. That area, typically at the base of the vagina, will become less sensitive eventually, but it may take a year or more. Find a position (use pillows if you have to) that angles your partner away from the scar. If you have very sharp pain, use a mirror to check your scar for a black line like a splinter – you may have a stitch that didn't dissolve, and it will need to be removed.

After a Caesarian, the biggest concern is the abdominal scar; any position that puts pressure on it is out.

## Milk Gets in Your Eyes

Sex can make your milk spray, because the hormone oxytocin, which triggers the let-down reflex, is released when you have an orgasm. This at best was distracting, and at worst used to make me laugh, grab for tissues and completely lose any romantic focus. The best way to handle it, if you don't like cold, wet sheets, is to wear a sleep bra with nursing pads. Also, try to feed the baby shortly beforehand (though you may leak anyway).

The optimal time window may take a while to work out. If your baby's been fed recently, he'll be more likely to give you some free time, and, if you're nursing, your breasts will be less likely to leak. But, for me anyway, it takes a certain amount of time to move from 'mama cow' mode to 'romantic lover' mode. (About a year or two.)

'The first time my ever-patient husband and I had sex,' said Sheila, 'I wore my nursing bra, with pads, so he wouldn't accidentally brush up against my breasts and start the milk fountain. I still leaked.'

## Get to Know Yourself Again

Of course, leaking milk effectively makes your breasts off limits. This was fine for me, because no matter how romantic I was feeling, in the first few months following the births of my children, I just couldn't stand to have my husband touch my breasts. This isn't unusual. I do find it ironic, however, that the one time in my life my breasts could fill out anything bigger than an A cup they were off limits. I just wish I had known at the time how common it was; that might have taken the edge off a number of tense muments.

'My breasts, and especially my nipples, definitely did not feel erotic to me,' Cecily said, 'but they were a big turn-on for my husband. This caused some frustration on both sides!'

There may be other parts of your body that you used to like to have touched, and suddenly don't. For Kerri, it was her stomach. 'I didn't want to be reminded of how much work I had ahead of me to tighten it up again,' she said.

All these new rules about what can and can't be touched will probably baffle your partner. But your body has been through some huge changes. Why would you expect everything to feel the same?

## Timing Is Everything

Complicating the whole sex thing even further is the probability that when you have an orgasm, or are about to, your baby will wake up. Anticipating her cry can ruin the most romantic mument. If you can get away for a few hours, do so.

**Think about birth control – you can get pregnant again before you've had your first postpartum period.**

If you really, really don't feel like sex, don't worry about it, but don't entirely forget about it. Reassure your partner as best you can, and make reservations for a romantic evening away a few days after your baby's first birthday.

## Hair Loss

The most upsetting physical change after the birth of my babies was when, it seemed, I started losing handfuls of hair every time I took a shower. For me, this occurred around the sixth or seventh month, but it usually starts a little earlier. It's normal; during pregnancy, the typical shedding cycle of hair changes. The good news is that, for a while when you're pregnant, your hair is thicker than ever. The bad news is that this too shall pass, and you'll lose the normal amount of hair you would have had you not been pregnant – all at once. This may be the time to think about cutting your hair short for a while. Losing short hair is not quite so traumatic somehow, and is a lot easier on the shower drain.

'My hair started falling out about four months after my babies were born,' Christina said. 'The first time I was terrified; but the second time I knew it was only temporary.'

'Not only did my hair all fall out at once, it all grew back at once, in a little fringe around my hairline,' reported Cecily. 'It was very difficult to style, and I still have an area of hair shorter than the rest.'

The time it takes for your hair to look 'normal' again depends on your hair's growth cycle, which can vary dramatically from woman to woman. Get a good haircut or some nice scarves and have faith; it will grow back.

## Getting Your Body Back

About six weeks after the birth, your uterus is pretty much back to where it was before the birth in terms of size and position. I say 'pretty much' because some things will never be back the way they were. Your uterus will always be a little larger than before, the opening of the cervix wider, and your pelvic muscles and ligaments will be looser.

Your body may not feel like yours. You just got used to having a huge stomach, and now it's relatively flat again, but loose and sagging. Your breasts have very little in common with the ones you were used to. Your waist and hips are wider and will probably stay that way, and don't expect your feet to return to their pre-pregnancy size. I had to move a lot of skirt buttons, and I had to throw out a lot of shoes.

'Even though I weigh less now than I did before my pregnancy, my body is much changed,' said Sheila. 'Above my Caesarian scar, which is permanently numb in spots, my belly juts out and sags down in a stretch-marked mess. No more bikinis in this lifetime. And now, almost a year after weaning my daughter, my right boob, which my daughter preferred, is smaller and sags more than the left one. It's just worn out, and looks it. I've now got a body that screams, "Look at me! I'm a Mummy!"'

While you may not get your old body back, you can get a body you like. Said Chris, 'I feel better about my body and sexier at nearly forty, having had two kids, than I ever did for the thirty-five years before their births. I swear my boobs are far better than they were before I had babies, and, after years of wearing one-piece bathing suits, I now think I look better in a bikini.'

If you're breast-feeding exclusively, you probably won't get your period for five or six months – and you may not get it for several years. Seems only fair, with all the other messes you've got to deal with. But don't count on it. I got my period back every time at six weeks, even though I was breast-feeding every three hours, day and night. Cecily was more average. With each of her births, her period returned exactly one month after she stopped breast-feeding.

## Body Work

If you haven't started exercising regularly before reading this, start now. There are a lot of good reasons to exercise – to stay healthy, to boost your mood, and to fit into your pre-pregnancy clothes again. For me, the most important reason was to get back in touch with my body – to put on, for an hour anyway, clothes I couldn't nurse in, look in the mirror, and recognize that the leg I was lifting was actually mine.

Immediately after the birth (or as soon as you have any feeling down in your pelvis) start pelvic floor exercises. Squeeze the muscles that control the flow of urine, hold for three seconds, and relax. Do at least 20 a day – and do them for the rest of your life. You can also start easy exercises for your lower back and abdomen, although you won't have much success even feeling where your abdominal muscles are for a week or two. Make sure, however, that you don't do any exercises that require you to be upside down until all bleeding stops (no shoulderstands, for example, if you're doing yoga), because blood flowing back into the still-open cervix can cause infection. Nurse just before you exercise; you'll be more comfortable, and the effect of exercise-induced lactic acid, which can make milk slightly sour, will have dissipated prior to the next feeding.

Breast-feeding, which uses about 500–1000 calories a day, will help you lose weight, but plan to drop the grams slowly. If you're thinking about dieting yourself back into shape, and you're significantly overweight, do so only by controlling your eating. Focus on eating reasonable portions of healthy foods at regular meals. If 'dieting' means a restrictive fad or starvation diet (living on protein drinks or grapefruit), don't – you'll threaten your baby's health as well as your own.

## Exercises with Baby

- **Fly a Kite:** Besides being great for your back and stomach, kite-flying can calm a gretful baby. Start out sitting, with your knees bent, feet flat on the floor. Position your baby's body face down against your lower legs and, stabilizing your baby with your hands, roll back, lifting your baby up with your legs. You can stay in that position, pressing the small of your back against the floor, or rock from side to side, to help release your back. You can gently lift and lower your baby with your legs to exercise your knee and leg muscles. Or you can do abdominal exercises by lifting your head and shoulders off the ground, reaching toward your baby with a kiss.
- **Straddle Stretches:** Sit with your legs in a V, and lay or sit your baby in the middle. Stretch to each side and to the middle, holding each stretch for at least 20 seconds without bouncing (go ahead and kiss your baby as much as you want).
- **Baby Presses (AKA reverse push-ups):** Lie on your back, knees bent, feet flat on the floor. Put your baby on your chest, holding him under his arms, and pressing your lower back against the floor, lift him slowly in the air above your face until your arms are almost straight.

FIGURE 18-1:
Fly a kite

FIGURE 18-2:
Straddle
stretches

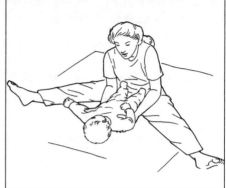

FIGURE 18-3:
Baby presses

FIGURE 18-4:
Pillow stretch

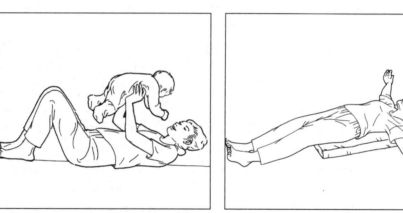

## Great Stretches for Any Time

- **Wall Stretch:** Stand facing a
  wall, about one step (or an arm's length) back, feet shoulder width
  apart. Put both hands flat against the wall at shoulder height. Bend
  over, passing your head between your elbows, pressing your back flat,
  parallel to the ground.
- **Pillow Stretch:**
  Lie on your back, with a pillow or couch bolster under your shoulders.
  Let your arms and shoulders relax back and tip your head back. This
  opens your chest, stretches the chest muscles, and counters the curved
  position you use while holding a baby.

## Baby Wrist

Given all the holding, cuddling and cradling that babies require, it's no surprise that some mothers suffer from a condition sometimes called baby wrist. This is a repetitive stress injury, characterized by pain or tingling in the wrist, that can cause long-term damage if not treated. A variation is pain around the thumb or fingers, which doctors used to think came from opening and closing safety pins while changing, but now associate with lifting and carrying the baby. The pain can increase at night, when the accumulation of fluid increases pressure on the nerves.

Don't start any form of impact exercise (running, aerobics) for at least six weeks. Your stretched muscles, tendons, and ligaments can't safely support your organs, and your cardiovascular system is still reverting to normal.

- If your lochia (post-childbirth discharge) turns red after exercising, you're doing too much.
- Don't jog or do any exercises that require bouncing with your baby in a carrier. (You can hold your baby in a frontpack, however, while walking or riding an exercisebike.)
- Don't use a baby jogger until around six months of age. Younger babies can risk neck injuries.

Michelle had a severe case of baby wrist when her son, Ben, was four or five months old. 'I had an agonizing pain in my left hand, from my mid-forearm to my fingers. I called the doctor in the middle of the night and said I thought I was having a heart attack.' The pain turned out to be from cupping her hand around her baby's head as she held him and his bottle in one arm, and responded to ice, ibuprofen, ultrasound therapy and exercise.

'I had mild tendonitis during the first several months of my daughter's life,' Sheila said. 'I periodically wore wrist braces, which helped the pain, as did the occasional cortisone injection.'

Baby wrist often begins with hormonal changes during pregnancy, which cause internal swelling in the wrist. It is aggravated by holding the infant with a bent wrist, as well as by changing, snapping little snaps, pushing a buggy and lugging a baby carrier. And nursing mothers tend to make the condition worse by curling their hands under their full breasts when they're asleep.

You can avoid the condition by stretching your wrists regularly and lifting light hand weights. Make sure you keep your wrists in a 'neutral' position (straight, but relaxed), when holding your baby. (My big mistakes were cupping my hand around my baby's head while nursing with my wrist at a 90-degree angle and pushing the buggy with my wrists bent.) If you've already got a case of baby wrist, put ice on the area a few times a day, and take ibuprofen to reduce inflammation. Wear a wrist brace designed for repetitive stress injuries whenever you can, which may only be when you sleep, since you can't pick up your baby while wearing it.

## My Aching Back

While you were pregnant, you began to carry yourself differently to balance your growing stomach. Continuing this new posture can strain your back, as can nursing (remember to use a nursing stool and bring your baby to your breast, rather than leaning over your baby) and the constant lifting and carrying a new baby needs.

'Back pain was constant for me,' said Natasha. 'Ice, heat and massage helped, as did learning careful lifting, bending and carrying techniques.'

To minimize the stress on your back, rediscover your correct posture. Stand in front of a mirror naked, and close your eyes. Rock from side to side, shrug your shoulders, take a slow, deep breath, and exhale. Then, without opening your eyes, try to find a centred position. Open your eyes and look in the mirror. Are your shoulders even? Is your bottom tipped up? Are your knees tilted in? To adjust your alignment, put your feet just under your hips, then tip your pelvis forward and back until you find its centre. Tuck in your bottom, and straighten your shoulders. You may need to do this a few times a day until you get used to your new centre.

Become aware of how you hold and handle your baby. When you bend down to pick her up, bend your knees, support her close to your chest and use your leg muscles to lift – don't lean over. The same goes for the car seat. Climb into the car as far as possible and lift your baby up against you before squirming backwards out of the car. Once your baby is too big for the sink or baby bath (which you can place on a counter), think about taking baths with your baby instead of leaning over the tub. When you are on the floor, changing a nappy or playing, squat or sit cross-legged to reduce awkward leaning.

**Why sleep with extra pillows?**
Sleep on your back with a pillow under your knees, or on your side with a pillow between your legs to preserve alignment and reduce additional stress.

Try to carry your baby in the centre of your body as much as possible, rather than on one hip. Or, if you carry your baby on your hip, change sides often (the same goes for carrying your baby in a sling). Regularly using your hip as a baby chair can, after a while, cause muscle and nerve damage that can take years to recover from.

CHAPTER 19

# Making Memories

When my first son was born, my husband and I took what we thought was a roll of photos of him lying on my hospital bed in a patch of sun. Some time after we got home, we found out that we hadn't put film in the camera. The promised photographs from the hospital photographer never arrived, and it was several weeks before we got our first camcorder.

## Paparazzi

To have a slightly more complete record of your baby's first year than I do, try some of these suggestions.

Photograph everything your baby does on a normal day, at regular intervals (three months, six months, nine months). Order double prints, save one set for the album, and use the other set to make a book for your baby. Or use a digital camera, remembering to download the photos onto your computer at regular intervals.

Regularly photograph your rapidly growing child with something that doesn't change in size. My son has several photos beside a stuffed Mickey Mouse that towered over him when he was born, and now looks tiny in his hands. Several mums have done the same thing with teddy bears. When my daughter was newborn, I began photographing her every few months in her older brother's toddler bed (now handed down to her), with her brother's infant-sized dolls on either side of her. In the first pictures it's hard to tell which figure is a sleeping baby and which one is a doll; now the dolls snuggle in the crook of her arms and her feet touch the end of the bed. You can also try 'baby in a hat', 'baby with the cat' or 'baby in Mum's chair'.

**Capture your baby's typical facial expressions, watching her face closely over several days, and take lots of pictures with her face filling the frame.**

Develop a photo series (these work with video as well). I haven't done anything yet with my baby-in-a-bed photos, but hope to frame a sequence of them someday. I'm also working on a 'girl with roses' series. Every year on my daughter's birthday, I photograph her with one rose for every year of her age.

'I unintentionally started a tradition on my daughter's first Easter,' said Leslie. 'I took pictures of my husband with her in the front garden in front of a rose bush that was in bloom. We've repeated that picture every year, since that bush always seems to be in bloom. And looking back, it is a nice chronicle of our daughter's growth.'

'I ended up with a pretty nice bath series, though it wasn't by design,' said Jessica. 'I call it "Splish Splash", and it's one of my favourite pages in her album, with photos from her very first bath – the one the nurses gave her at the hospital – all the way to her graduation to the big bathtub.'

Don't put the camera away when your child is crying or screaming. Tears and tantrums are a big part of the first year – and many years to come – and though you may think you'll want to forget them, someday you'll treasure those photos.

Don't forget to get pictures with each parent. In most couples one person takes on the photographer role, and sometimes finds out when it is too late that he or she is missing from the photographic record.

Videotape and photograph the significant people in your child's life – grandparents, other relatives, the neighbour's baby who he sees every day at the park, your regular babysitter.

You don't need to save every work of art once your baby starts scribbling, scrawling and painting; you'll quickly be overwhelmed. Instead, save a representative sample, and regularly surround your child by her artwork and take a photo.

## Keepsakes: Beyond the Photo

When your baby says her first word – or even babbles regularly – try getting her voice on tape. Introduce each segment by stating the date, place and activity, then get her talking or laughing by making silly faces or pointing to pictures in a book. Your computer can be better than a tape recorder (particularly since audio tapes can get lost in a drawer in a muddle of other tapes). Plug in a microphone (yours may have come with one built in), and use whatever recording software you have on hand. On my Macintosh, I accessed my sound control panel and changed my computer's alert sound from a beep to my baby saying 'Uh-oh'. (Make sure you keep a copy of these files whenever you upgrade computers.)

**tips**

Don't forget the power of the pen. Keep a birthday journal and write your child a birthday letter in a blank book (available at stationery shops). Start with his birth story and include important family and news events that occurred in the months around his birth. Then update it yearly, with a letter describing his achievements over the year, relating a funny story, detailing major family changes, and reviewing the world news. Keep it a secret, and turn it over to him as a senior-school-leaving present.

Write in the front of your child's favourite books, the ones that you end up reading every night. Put down her name, her age and anything striking about the book (that she always pointed to the lamp in *Good Night Moon* and said 'light', for example, or that 'moon' was her third word).

Keep a journal, recording anything that comes to mind. 'The best thing we've been doing is keeping a book and pen on our bedside table,' said Katrin. 'Weeks may go by and we don't write anything in it, but it's there when something special happened during the day. We've done it from the beginning and love reading what we have written so far. There is so much stuff we would completely forget otherwise.'

If a journal sounds too daunting, keep a calendar. I put mine above the changing table, with a pen handy. Then you can jot down notes each day, and transfer the information to a baby book later. (Later, for me, turned out to be when I was pregnant with my next child. This, of course, means that child number three will never have a baby book.)

'Keeping a calendar allowed me to be sloppy with documentation,' said Jessica. 'I knew I'd never write anything in her baby book because I'd want it to look just right, but I allowed myself sloppy handwriting and cryptic statements on the calendar. This way, at least, I wrote things down. Naturally, I plan to transcribe it all neatly into her baby book. Someday.'

## Growth Charts

Start the classic growth chart - the marks on a door frame – as soon as your baby is standing on her own. Pick a regular time of year to update it, such as your child's birthday, New Year or another date you'll remember.

Make a footprint picture. Buy several extra-large sheets of acid-free watercolour paper and a bottle of roll-on stamp pad ink. Fold a paper towel a few times and roll ink onto it. Press your baby's foot first on the inked towel and then firmly onto the paper, starting on one edge and rolling the foot to make the print. Repeat with the other foot. Add a set of footprints every year or so, and by the time your child is in nursery school you'll be ready to frame these tracks of his growth. If your baby has older siblings, stamp their footprints side by side. (You can try handprints, too, but most babies will clench their hands up; footprints are a lot easier.)

If you go to the beach in the summer, on one of your outings bring along a box of dry plaster and a jug of tap water. When the tide is going out, pick a patch of damp sand, smooth it out, and stamp your baby's feet into it. Mix the plaster in a sand pail according to instructions, and pour it into the footprints. Wash out the sand pail immediately, or the plaster becomes impossible to remove.) You can pick the 'feet' up in about ten minutes; they will dry completely overnight. Tuck a loop of wire or string into each footprint just after you pour the plaster if you plan to hang them on the wall, or use them as they are, to make a path in your garden.

## First Birthday

The first birthday is not only about your baby. A one-year-old does not understand the concept of birthdays. This first birthday is also about you; it's a celebration of surviving your first year of motherhood. Yes, you are going to want to sing 'Happy Birthday' to your baby, blow out his candle and then feed him a slice of cake with gooey icing – if only for the photo opportunity – but beyond that, make this *your* party.

One woman I know celebrated her babies' first birthdays by inviting all the women who had participated in the births to a restaurant lunch, leaving the kids at home with her husband (the cake and candles came later). She reasoned that since birth was a rite of passage for a woman, who better to celebrate that with than other women? The group included her midwife, paeditrician and best friend, and the party honoured her birth as a mother. My friend Pat invited a host of friends and their children to a 'bubble party' – soap bubbles for the kids and champagne bubbles for the adults – to celebrate her survival of what had been, because of the death of her husband, an unbelievably challenging first year.

Think about what would make this celebration meaningful for you.

'Recognizing that the first birthday is more a celebration for parents— along the lines of "Whew, we made it!" – than for the child, we had a garden barbecue for family and friends,' Leslie said. 'It was a way to reconnect with friends we hadn't seen for a while because we had just been too busy, and for everyone to see our daughter Grace without a lot of pressure on her.'

Sing another song in addition to 'Happy Birthday', decorate the table with your child's birth flower, propose a toast to your partner. (But not too many – Joy's second and third children were both conceived after guests went home from her first daughter's birthday parties.)

Don't expect your child to open gifts in an orderly manner. I know you want to see what's in them, but your one-year-old may happily play with the wrapped boxes for days without losing interest – why push it?

Begin your personal celebration with the moment you went into labour. You'll probably be remembering that time anyway, so be conscious of it. Watch the clock, and, no matter how busy your day is, take a few muments to remember what it felt like physically and emotionally when you realized this baby was about to be born. I find myself glancing at the clock throughout the day, remembering, 'Oh, this is when I was walking on the beach, having contractions every five minutes, and this was when I was in the shower at the hospital.' When your child is two or three, you can involve him in this tradition by telling him his birth story on the eve of his birthday. You may find that the 'when I was born' bedtime story becomes a favourite.

## Quotable Mum

Jenny wrote this letter for her daughter Abbey's first birthday. She plans to write Abbey a letter every year.

Dear Abbey,

One year ago at this moment I was lying in the bath, trying to relax through powerful contractions that lasted ninety seconds and came every three minutes. My memory of that day is a bit vague on some points – I think it was cold like today, and I'm pretty sure we'd had a lot of snow already – but there are some things I'll never forget. I won't forget the moment that morning, lying in bed browsing through seed catalogues after a post-pancake nap (the pancakes having been eaten at the suggestion of your Aunt Lynne, who recommended carbohydrates as my due date neared), when I realized I'd been having what felt like menstrual cramps. I'll never forget sitting at my desk answering e-mails and doing odd bits of work, with a sheet of paper next to me where I jotted down the time and duration of each contraction. Or that moment, at around 3 PM, when I finally decided that this was real and called Fred (you know him as Daddy). He came racing home immediately.

A year ago tonight, at about 11, we called the doctor. He said to come to the hospital, but we said we wanted to wait. As soon as I put the phone down, I changed my mind and told Fred I wanted to go, NOW. The contractions were two minutes apart – why wait any more? I'd spent all day breathing and rocking. I'd crouched backwards over the chair during *ER* – I don't THINK it was the episode where the young woman dies in childbirth, but I can't be sure. I'd eaten a big bowl of lentil soup to make sure I'd stay strong. And off we went.

A year ago today there was no baby, sleeping fitfully in the bedroom after a day with a nasty cold. Back then I didn't know the meaning of sleep deprivation, and I had no idea 'ba' could mean so many different things. I didn't have a house full of primary-coloured plastic objects, and had vowed that I never would. I didn't know anything about the family bed, pelvic floor exercises, breast pumps or nasal aspirators (yuck).

By 1:30 AM I was in the birth tub. We brought dozens of CDs to listen to but the only one I wanted then was by Abbey Lincoln. That's where you get your name.

By 2:30 AM I was out of the tub and enduring the most excruciating pain I'd ever experienced, along with the greatest exhilaration. I remember the moment when I realized I'd made it past the point of no return – even if I wanted to have medication, it was too late. Then there was the moment when I knew it was hurting as much as it ever would – and you were just about out. I'd done it.

The next part I don't remember so well. I can recall my first look at you, lying on my stomach, looking back at me. I remember singing Gershwin songs to soothe you, for you were crying, and to soothe me while they sewed me up. It gets even more blurred after that – I can picture the hospital room, the nurses, the balloons and the visitors, but when I try to conjure an image of the baby, all I can see is the bright-eyed one-year-old you are now. Why is that? The part I want to remember most, holding onto that tiny newborn baby, has been eclipsed by the moment to moment reality of now, this little girl who lives in my house and rules my world. Luckily, I have lots of pictures, but it's funny how in my memory you looked perfectly perfect, not like a red-faced, squashed-up newborn baby at all. But in the pictures, you look like a red-faced, squashed-up newborn baby! Just like how in my memory, you were endlessly fascinating, doing something new and different every moment, but in my videos you were an amoeba who basically just lay there like every other newborn.

Abbey, you are one year old today. You are a totally walking girl. You make a joyful sound (like a creaky door) whenever the kitty walks in the room, and pat your legs like you've seen me do to call her over. Whenever you spot your toothbrush, you make a brushing motion with your fingers on your teeth. You are shy with strangers unless they ignore you, then you lean over and bat your eyelashes until they smile. You like to make funny faces, especially a scowl with your eyes rolled back – we call it 'the look'. You say 'a-ma' for mummy, 'dee' for cat, 'va' for wolf, 'ba' for ball and light, 'beh' for bear, and 'abloo' for just about everything else, especially water and apple sauce.

I haven't changed as much as I'd hoped. I dreamed I'd become more focused and present, that I'd be more in the moment, that I'd stop rushing from one thing to the next in my slapdash way. I have, a little, but I'm still me, and still fighting that urge to always be DOING something. Once in a while I remember to just sit down and enjoy being with you. (I think you bite me when you nurse as your way of reminding me that this time will soon be gone forever, so stop doing twenty other things all the time and PAY ATTENTION!)

On to year two!

All my love,

Mummy

## The Best Part: Baby's First Year

What better way to conclude your first year as a new mum than by sharing these special quotes from your peers? Maybe they'll inspire you to make your own 'Best Part' journal entry.

'The best part of the first year was. . . everything! Even if, in the mument, it was terrible and I thought I was going to go crazy or burst into tears, when I look back, it was either comical or just wonderful. From Alex's first smile and laugh, to his first steps, and everything in between. I never knew I could love someone so much!' – *Kerri*

'Being a mother is the hardest job I have ever loved. I did not know it was possible to love a person in the way and to the depth that I love my daughter. Even when I felt exhausted and frustrated in that first year, I would tiptoe into her room before I went to bed to gaze upon her beautiful, sleeping face, and my heart would overflow with love every time.' – *Mary*

'Becoming a mother was like coming into my own. I knew that from the moment of birth that it was something I was created for. It completed me and allowed me to love in a capacity I'd never experienced before. I felt a bond with my Creator as I cooperated in this miracle. I grew up and finally apart from my own mother more so through parenthood than through marriage. I had to finally let go of many of my own fears in order to be secure on behalf of my child. And as a long-time sufferer from a painful disease, I finally was able to watch my body behave as it had been intended to, and to behave powerfully and naturally. It was the highlight of my life.' – *Alissa*

'The best part of the first year was when our kids first recognized us. Picking them up from babysitters and seeing their faces light up because they recognized Mum or Dad. And hearing the babies' first laughs. And having a baby fall asleep on my shoulder was precious. There are so many special muments in the first year, and sometimes you forget how special they are.' – *Glorianne*

'The best part of the first year was looking at the joy and love in my husband's eyes every time he looked at our son.' – *Kathryn*

'The best moment in that first year was holding my newborn twins right after they came out. There hasn't been much in my whole life that has exceeded the incredible feeling of that mument.' – *Moira*

'The best thing about the first year was becoming part of the "club". Suddenly I had something in common with all the other women, regardless of where they work or how much money they made. I also took on a different attitude: "Hey, I gave birth; anything else pales in comparison."' – *Leslie R*

'The best memory of my first year is of my husband and me holding our sleeping baby, tears in our eyes, while listening to Emmylou Harris softly singing "Child of Mine".' – *Sue*

'The best thing was seeing the wonder on my daughter's face over the most ordinary things, like coloured lights, a tiny insect on the ground, a beautiful red leaf or a muddy puddle. She made me slow down to appreciate all the little gifts we come across all day long.' – *Julie*

'The best thing is that after all the sleepless nights and frustration at the beginning about a colicky baby, at the end you get some love back, just a little hug, cuddle or kiss, that is everything you ever needed.' – *Esther*

'The best part was watching Francis grow from a wailing bundle of reactions and needs into a walking, talking, communicating creature." – *Adrienne*

'Successful nursing was the most difficult goal for me, but it ended up being my favourite thing. I miss it.' – *Sheila*

'The best moment of the first year was when my son, Chris, was about a week old. I took him with me to the petrol station, and while I was filling the car, a woman came over and said, "I see you have a new baby." I smiled, and she continued, "Don't you feel like someone turned on the lights and now it's clear to you what life is all about?" She was so right!' – *Lynne*

'The best part was watching my child become a person who was showing signs of being able to think and reason.' – *Jessica*

'The best part of the first year was learning about this new person in my life, learning about what made my baby smile, cry, laugh and cuddle.' – *Lisa*

'My best part of the first year was the laughter a baby brings. Before parenthood, it was quiet and settled in my home. There was not so much laughter, not so much to actually smile about. That was the best change.' – *Ursula*

'The best part for me was watching this little being grow from a helpless newborn about whom I knew almost nothing into a real little person with her distinct personality, looks, abilities, preferences, and interests.' – *Cecily*

'The best thing was seeing my child grow and be healthy. I nursed both my kids the first year, and this was a huge accomplishment for me.' – *Lynn*

'The best moment came a couple of months after we had Sophia. We visited a friend who had to buzz us in to enter her apartment. When she answered the buzzer, I said, "It's the Blums." There was something about that that caught me. We were more of a family. Before that I might have said, "It's Jodi and Jeff", but now we were "the Blums".' – *Jodi*

'The best thing about the first year was the incredible love I felt for my son, his first laugh, and the joy of seeing him grow from a newborn baby into a little toddler. What an experience! I wouldn't change it for anything in the world.' – *Kim*

'The best part of the first year – all three times – were the gummy smiles just for me.' – *Julia*

'I think the best thing about the first year is realizing the true definition of unconditional love. It is astonishing how fiercely and passionately you fall in love with this tiny creature that can do nothing for you in return, other than need you completely and reciprocate your love in full. You can't remember life without her – or what you remember seems incomplete. Every smile, every gurgle, every coo brings immeasurable joy. There is nothing you wouldn't do for her, no need to say no to any wish she might have (yet), and no feeling of peace quite like the one you get when she falls asleep on your shoulder, blowing her warm baby breath on your neck.

'These are the memories you keep of that first year. Long after the labour and delivery, tantrums and sleepless nights have faded into ancient history, the infant that you alone can see every time you look at that toddler/schoolchild/teenager/adult is the gift of that first magical year.' – *Leslie B*

# Appendix A
# Charts

# Health History

Information you and anyone else taking care of the baby will need to have on hand. Start keeping track of it now.

Date of birth, name of hospital, doctors: _____

_____

Weight, length, head size: _____

Any congenital problems: _____

_____

_____

Complications during pregnancy or delivery: _____

_____

_____

_____

How long breast-fed: _____

Food allergies: _____

_____

_____

_____

Drug allergies: _____

_____

_____

_____

# Health History (continued)

Chronic conditions (frequent ear infections, asthma, other): _____

_____

_____

_____

Major medical treatments (surgeries or hospitalizations): _____

_____

_____

_____

Vaccinations: _____

_____

_____

_____

Illnesses: _____

_____

_____

_____

Date of onset: _____          Date of onset: _____

Date of recovery: _____          Date of recovery: _____

Diagnosis: _____          Diagnosis: _____

Medications given: _____          Medications given: _____

Reactions to medication: _____          Reactions to medication: _____

# My Baby's Milestones

Claps: _____

Grabs a toy or object: _____  What? _____

Rolls over: _____

Sits unsupported: _____

Crawls, creeps, or somehow crosses the room: _____

Pulls up to standing: _____  On what? _____

Walks: _____  How many steps? _____

Climbs out of crib: _____

Runs: _____

Smiles: _____  At what? _____

Laughs out loud: _____  At what? _____

Shows excitement: _____  At what? _____

Shows anger: _____  At what? _____

Has a favourite toy: _____  What is it? _____

Coos or oohs (vowels): _____  What did it sound like? _____

Babbles (consonants): _____  What sounds are the favourites? _____

Babbles without repeating syllables: _____  What did it sound like? _____

First word: _____  Word? _____

Second word: _____  Word? _____

First animal sound: _____  What animal? _____

List all the words your baby can say on his or her first birthday: _____

_____

# New Mum Milestones

Record (and celebrate!) these stellar events in your new life as a mum.

First time you have sex: _____

First time you like it: _____

First postpartum menstrual period: _____

First outing without your baby: _____

_____

_____

How long? _____ Baby stayed with whom? _____

First outing without worrying about your baby: _____

_____

_____

First evening out with your partner: _____

_____

_____

Five consecutive hours of sleep: _____

Seven consecutive hours of sleep: _____

First overnight stay away from baby: _____

_____

Returning to work: _____

First weekend away: _____

_____

## APPENDIX B

# Exercise Primer

## Just After the Birth

- **Kegels:** Tighten your vaginal and pelvic muscles (as if stopping a stream of urine), hold for three seconds, and relax. Do five repetitions every hour or so for the first few days to increase blood circulation to the area and promote healing.
- **Tummy Tighteners:** Lie on the bed, inhale, and slowly exhale through pursed lips while you tighten your abdominal muscles as much as you can. Repeat five times.
- **Chin to Chests:** Lie flat on the bed (without a pillow) and slowly lift your head and touch your chin to your chest; you should feel your lower abdominal muscles tighten. Repeat five times.
- **Pelvic Rocks:** Lie on the floor, knees bent, feet flat, and tighten your abs while tucking your bottom under, pressing your lower back into the floor. Then relax, letting your back curve. Repeat five times.

## Abdominal Exercises

After a C-section, don't do any abdominal exercises until the incision has healed completely. (The incision may, however, still feel numb.)

FIGURE APP-1:
Curl-ups

FIGURE APP-2:
Side reaches

Before starting any abdominal exercises, check for diatasis, or separation of the recti abdominis muscles. Lie down, with knees bent and feet on the floor. With the finger of one hand, feel just below your navel for the soft indentation between the two bands of stomach muscles. Exhale as you lift

your head and shoulders and see how many fingers fit into the indentation—
if it's more than two and a half, do only the first three exercises.

- **Diastasis Corrector:** Lie on your back, knees bent, feet flat on floor.
  Push muscles in center of abdomen together while you exhale and
  slowly lift your head.
- **Leg Slides:** Lie on back with bent knees, feet flat. Slowly slide legs out
  until straight while pressing the lower back to the floor, then return to
  bent position.
- **Shoulder Lifts:** Lie down, knees bent. With your fingers stretching
  toward your toes, raise your head and shoulders off of the bed. Repeat
  five times.
- **Curl-ups:** Start with shoulder lifts, but come a little further, reaching
  between your knees, until your back begins to lift. Repeat five times.
- **Side Reaches:** Just like curl-ups, but reach to the outside of one knee
  for five reps, and then to the outside of the other knee for five more.

## Hand and Wrist Exercises

- **Wrist Rolls:** Stretch your arms forward and rotate wrists in one
  direction and then the other. Repeat ten times.
- **Wrist Lifts:** Place your forearm on a table, palm up, and wrist and
  hand hanging over the edge (first position). Hold a light weight (or
  can of soup) in your hand, and curl your wrist slowly up toward your
  arm (second position), and then slowly down. Repeat ten times.

FIGURE APP-3(a):
Wrist lift
(first position)

FIGURE APP-3(b):
Wrist lift
(second
position)

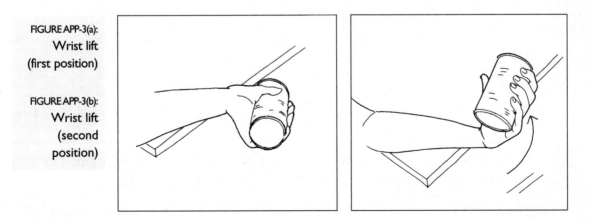

FIGURE APP-4(a):
Wrist roll
(first position)

FIGURE APP-4(b):
Wrist roll
(second
position)

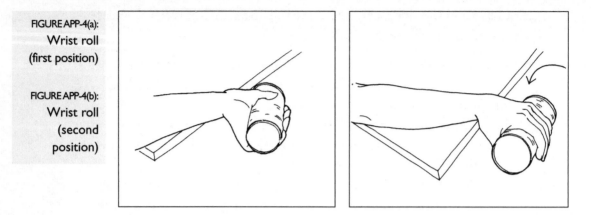

- **Wrist Twists:** Again, with your forearm on a flat surface, palm up, wrist and hand hanging over the edge (first position), hold one end of the weight or can and turn your hand slowly until your palm faces down (second position); then rotate back. Repeat ten times.

## Back Exercises

FIGURE APP-5(a):
Cat back
(first position)

FIGURE APP-5(b):
Cat back
(second
position)

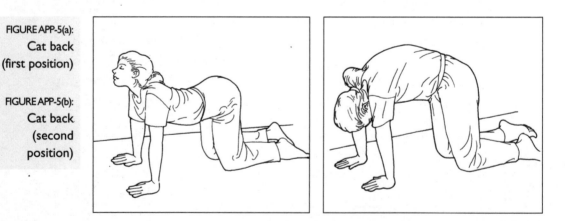

- **Cat Back:** Position yourself on your hands and knees, arms directly below your shoulders, knees directly below your hips. Drop the center of your back toward the floor, inhaling. On the exhale, arch your back up. Repeat ten times slowly. Remember to breathe.

FIGURE APP-6:
Wall sits

FIGURE APP-7:
Crocodile

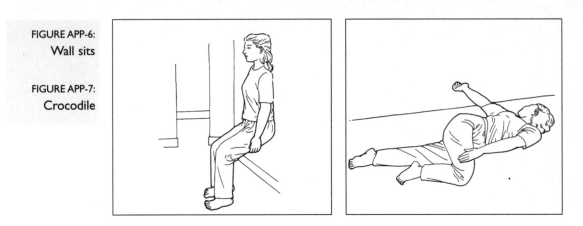

- **Wall Sits:** With feet shoulder-width apart and knees slightly bent, stand with your back against the wall, pressing the small of your back into the wall. Slowly lower yourself until your thighs are parallel to the floor, keeping your back pressed against the wall.
- **Crocodile:** Another yoga position. Start on your back, legs straight. Bend your right leg and rest the sole of that foot on the left knee, and scoot your hips slightly towards the right. Roll over to the left, your right knee dropping on the floor, arms reaching straight out in front of your face. Holding the right knee down with the left leg, turn the upper body and reach the right arm around in the opposite direction.
- **Knee Hug:** Lying on your back, pull your knees into your chest and wrap your arms around your legs. Rock from side to side.
- **Child's Pose:** For this yoga position, rest on your knees, in the 'cat back' position. Slowly bring your hips back and down toward your heels, folding your stomach across your thighs and knees, until your forehead touches the ground. Depending on your flexibility, you can slowly bring your arms to the side, or bend them at the elbows and stack your hands under your head. Stay, breathing slowly, as long as the position feels comfortable.

# Index